Chicago P.   Library
Avalon B
8148 S. Stony Island Ave.
Chicago, IL 60617

Drugs

DISCARD

Other Books of Related Interest

Teen Decisions Series
Alcohol
Dating
Gangs
Pregnancy
Sex
Smoking
Violence

Opposing Viewpoints Series
Addiction
AIDS
Alcohol
American Values
Chemical Dependency
Crime and Criminals
Culture Wars
Drug Abuse
Gangs
Teens at Risk
Tobacco and Smoking
Violence
The War on Drugs

Current Controversies Series
Crime
Drug Trafficking
Illegal Drugs
Teen Addiction
Teens and Alcohol

Contemporary Issues Companions
Marijuana
Teen Addiction
Teen Alcoholism
Teen Smoking

At Issue Series
Heroin
Legalizing Drugs
Marijuana

Drugs

William Dudley, *Book Editor*

Daniel Leone, *President*
Bonnie Szumski, *Publisher*
Scott Barbour, *Managing Editor*

Greenhaven Press Inc., San Diego, California

No part of this book may be reproduced or used in any form or by any means, electrical, mechanical, or otherwise, including, but not limited to, photocopy, recording, or any information storage and retrieval system, without prior written permission from the publisher.

Every effort has been made to trace owners of copyrighted material.

Library of Congress Cataloging-in-Publication Data

Drugs / William Dudley, book editor.
    p. cm. — (Teen decisions)
    Includes bibliographical references and index.
    ISBN 0-7377-0922-7 (pbk. : alk. paper) —
    ISBN 0-7377-0923-5 (lib. : alk. paper)
    1. Teenagers—Drug use. 2. Drug abuse—Prevention. 3. Drug abuse—Treatment. 4. Narcotic habit—Treatment. I. Dudley, William, 1964– II. Series.

HV5824.Y68 D78 2002
362.29—dc21   2001040780

Cover photo: © Spencer Grant/PhotoEdit

© 2002 by Greenhaven Press, Inc.
10911 Technology Place, San Diego, CA 92127

Printed in the U.S.A.

R0411678569

Contents

Chicago Public Library
Avalon Branch
8148 S. Stony Island Ave.
Chicago, IL 60617

Chapter 3: Consequences of Using and Abusing Drugs

Chapter 4: Addiction and Recovery

Chapter 5: Making Decisions About Drugs and Your Life

Foreword

The teen years are a time of transition from childhood to adulthood. By age 13, most teenagers have started the process of physical growth and sexual maturation that enables them to produce children of their own. In the United States and other industrialized nations, teens who have entered or completed puberty are still children in the eyes of the law. They remain the responsibility of their parents or guardians and are not expected to make major decisions themselves. In most of the United States, eighteen is the age of legal adulthood. However, in some states, the age of majority is nineteen, and some legal restrictions on adult activities, such as drinking alcohol, extend until age twenty-one.

This prolonged period between the onset of puberty and the achieving of legal adulthood is not just a matter of hormonal and physical change, but a learning process as well. Teens must learn to cope with influences outside the immediate family. For many teens, friends or peer groups become the basis for many of their opinions and actions. In addition, teens are influenced by TV shows, advertising, and music.

The *Teen Decisions* series aims at helping teens make responsible choices. Each book provides readers with thought-provoking advice and information from a variety of perspectives. Most of the articles in these anthologies were originally written for, and in many cases by, teens. Some of the essays focus on ethical and moral dilemmas, while others present pertinent legal and scientific information. Many of the articles tell personal stories about decisions teens have made and how their lives were affected.

One special feature of this series is the "Points of Contention," in which specially paired articles present directly opposing views on controversial topics. Additional features in each book include a listing of organizations to contact for more information, as well as a bibliography to aid readers interested in more information. The *Teen Decisions* series strives to include both trustworthy information and multiple opinions on topics important to teens, while respecting the role teens play in making their own choices.

Introduction

"You hear about drugs all the time. In school, you learn that using any kind of drugs—even cigarettes and alcohol—isn't really good for you. But from the way some kids talk about drugs, you still get kind of curious."

Kim, age 13

Drugs are chemicals that affect the human body, including the brain. Many drugs are taken for medical reasons, such as to combat disease, relieve pain, or treat depression. Others are used for nonmedical reasons—often simply for the experience of having a chemical substance alter one's feelings and perceptions. Drug abuse occurs when a person uses drugs in a way that interferes with a productive and healthy life. It is a serious problem that affects millions of Americans.

American Drug Policy

Making decisions about nonmedical drugs is something both individuals and societies do. One way society expresses its decisions is through its laws—those written formal rules of behavior that are enforced by the criminal justice system. Through its laws, American society has made certain pronouncements about drugs. Some substances, such as nicotine (the main drug in tobacco products) and alcohol, are legal for adults to consume, but not for minors. Other substances, such as caffeine (a stimulant found in coffee and cola drinks) are permitted even for young people. But many drugs have been placed off limits. They are legally obtainable only with a doctor's prescription, or not at all.

Drug prohibition is a relatively recent phenomenon. Cocaine and heroin were both freely available in the nineteenth century;

federal laws controlling these substances date from 1914. Alcohol was legal for most of American history except between 1919 and 1933, when it was forbidden by the Eighteenth Amendment to the U.S. Constitution (a period known as Prohibition). Marijuana was banned by federal law in 1937, but became widely popular among young people in the 1960s and 1970s, leading some lawmakers to suggest its decriminalization. But since then public attitudes towards illegal drugs have hardened. In what has been called the "war on drugs," federal, state, and local governments have poured ever-increasing resources into preventing illegal drugs from entering the country and imprisoning people caught using and distributing drugs.

Some people have questioned this trend in U.S. drug policy. They argue that it is wrong for society to place restrictions on what individuals do to themselves, including changing their consciousness via chemicals. Despite the debate over the war on drugs, the war itself shows little sign of ending. The hard fact remains that the decision to use most kinds of recreational drugs necessarily involves a decision to break the law.

For many teens and adults, the fact that drug use is against the law is enough reason to avoid it. They may do so because they believe in obeying the law, or because they want to avoid the consequences of getting caught and punished. These consequences can be severe. They include expulsion from school, driver's license suspension, the loss of college financial aid, the forfeiture of cars or other property, and the denial of work opportunities. Perhaps the most serious repercussion is possible imprisonment. Your chances of being put in prison depend in part on your age (penalties are much harsher for people 18 and over), the circumstances of arrest, the drugs in question, and the state in which you live. In New Jersey, for example, people convicted as adults for distributing even a small amount of marijuana (with or without money changing hands) are sentenced to one year of prison without parole. Juveniles fourteen years and over can be tried and convicted as adults if charged with drug-related offenses in that state. Federal law mandates five-year prison sentences for people, including first-time offenders, caught and convicted as adults for possessing five grams of crack cocaine.

Extent of Drug Use

However, the illegality of drug use has not prevented many drugs from being readily available to teens, and has certainly not deterred all teens from trying drugs. According to the 1999 National Household Survey on Drug Abuse, an annual nationwide survey among Americans age twelve and older, about 14.8 million Americans admitted to using an illicit drug at least once during the month prior to being interviewed. The Monitoring the Future Study, an annual survey of drug use among youths, found that in 2000, 54 percent of surveyed high school seniors had tried illegal drugs at some point in their lives; almost a quarter of them had used drugs within the previous month. The most popular drugs for youth (besides alcohol and tobacco) were marijuana and inhalants (substances that give off chemical fumes that can affect the brain and are often found in household products such as solvents and glues).

Why do teens choose to defy the law when it comes to drugs? Many discount the possibility of getting caught, or perhaps are not fully aware of the legal consequences. Others are influenced by friends, romantic partners, or even parents or other family members who condone drugs and may be users themselves. Such immediate influences may often count for more than society's abstract prohibition through its laws. Many teens are avid consumers of pop culture, which often broadcasts messages glamorizing drug use. For some teens, the benefits promised by drugs—stress or pain relief, the removal of social inhibitions, the desire to fit in with friends, the pleasure many people claim to receive from altering their consciousness with drugs—outweigh the legal consequences as they see them. Adolescence is

also a time when many resent being told what to do by others—
the fact that drugs are prohibited may make them more enticing.

In making decisions about drugs, you should consider more
than the mere legal consequences of illegal drug use. You should
ask yourself why society has chosen to make certain drugs illegal. The effects of drugs can vary greatly depending on the particular drug and the circumstances of its use. But in too many instances, drugs are not beneficial or benign. The negative
consequences of drug use can be placed into three broad (and in-
terrelated) categories: health hazards, the risk of addiction, and
interference with the process of growing up and attaining a ful-
filling life.

Dangers to Health

Illegal drugs (and legal drugs that are misused) have a range of
potentially harmful effects to the body and the brain. In the most
extreme cases, experimenting with illegal drugs can lead to sudden death. While such cases are relatively rare, they are not unknown. Len Bias, a college basketball star, died of heart failure
in 1986 following a cocaine overdose. In January 1999 high
school student Samantha Reid died after she was "scooped"—
someone had secretly slipped the drug GHB (gamma-hydroxy-
butyrate) into her drink. Sara Aeschlimann, a few weeks before
high school graduation in 2000, died after taking a pill she
thought was ecstasy but which turned out to be PMA, a more
powerful substance. Between 1996 and 1999, Plano, an affluent
Texas suburb, suffered through the deaths of nineteen young
people reportedly due to heroin overdoses.

More commonly, using and abusing drugs can lead to nonfatal
results. Depending on the drug and how often it is used, a person risks various long- and short-term ailments. Regular marijuana use can lead to lung disease and impaired memory. Cocaine increases blood pressure, which may lead to strokes. The
hallucinogen ecstasy has been linked to long-term brain damage

that can affect a person's personality. Using drugs that need to be injected carries the risk of catching hepatitis or AIDS from infected needles.

Because their bodies are still developing, teens can be especially vulnerable to the cumulative effects of drugs. A person's physical or sexual development may be stunted. The immune system, lungs, heart, brain, liver, and other parts and functions of the body may be irreversibly harmed in ways that might not be fully understood until years later.

Addiction

The harmful effects of drugs increase if a person becomes addicted. A person is addicted if he or she is unable to stop craving or using a drug. Typically, the person needs more and more of the substance to recapture the "high" of the first use, and their life centers around obtaining and using the addictive drug. "Without experiencing addiction yourself," writes psychotherapist John Hicks, "you may find it almost impossible to understand the power that addiction has over a person's thinking, personality, and life."

Addiction has both psychological and physical aspects. Some drugs, such as heroin and amphetamines, are physically addictive—the body suffers without continued use of the drug. In other cases, the dependence is more psychological than physical—a person needs the drug to feel good about herself or to avoid feeling bad. Erika, a recovering addict, provides an example of the latter form of addiction in the following description of how her marijuana use increased during middle school:

> All I know is that it started progressing—it was almost out of my control. People say that pot's not addictive, but from my point of view, it definitely is. You get depressed once the high starts to wear off. The more stoned you get, the harder you hit when you come down.

Whether a drug becomes physically or psychologically addictive (or a combination of both), the results can be devastating for addicted individuals and those around them. In many cases, addiction can only be stopped through therapy and treatment programs.

Interfering with Growth

The emotional and social development of teens is also at risk when drugs enter the picture. The teen years can be a rewarding time as teens make more choices in how they live, explore who they are, plan their futures, and learn how to get along with others. However, these same challenges can make adolescence a stressful time, and many teens who have low self-esteem or feel stressed out may use drugs to cope with how they feel. Drugs can offer the illusion of help in that they can make a person feel better temporarily. However, drugs by themselves don't solve problems; they often simply hide them. When a drug's effects wear off, the feelings and problems remain.

Drugs can harm the development of teens in other ways as well. They can cause teens to withdraw from their family and from their friends who do not share an interest in drugs. In some cases, drugs can be a cause of serious family conflict. School grades may fall as teens lose interest in learning. The time and effort spent on obtaining and using drugs can detract from other activities, including school studies, reading, hobbies, or simply hanging out with friends—activities that are ultimately more conducive to healthy growth than taking drugs.

Perhaps one of the most insidious effects of drug use is its interference with the ability to make and learn from decisions. Hicks notes that the process of maturation itself largely consists of making choices, experiencing successes and failures from those choices, and learning from these experiences to make new choices. "People can grow both from their successes and failures as long as they are willing to take responsibility for the consequences of their actions," he argues. But "this learning process doesn't work as well when a young person makes the choice to use alcohol or other drugs" because drugs themselves can impair the brain's ability to process information and to learn. As author Wendy Maas states:

> Studies have shown that when young people use drugs, they lose the ability to learn through trial and error. The errors just don't register, and the teenager doesn't learn. If a seventeen-year-old has been using drugs since age 13, he or she may now be left with the emotional make-up of a thirteen-year-old.

Deciding About Drugs

All of these potential consequences of drug use—legal, health, and developmental—make drugs a critical area of choice for all teens. The essays in *Teen Decisions: Drugs* are not meant to be the final word on drugs, but may help you explore and consider some aspects of illicit drugs and the consequences of using them. Many are written by teens or describe the personal stories of young people who have tried drugs. In Chapter One, The Lure of Drugs, articles and personal anecdotes explain various reasons why some teens choose to try drugs. In Chapter Two, Some Facts About Drugs, basic information is provided about some of the currently popular drugs and what they can do to your brain and body. Chapter Three, Consequences of Using and Abusing Drugs, explores various health, legal, and social ramifications of drug use. Chapter Four, Addiction and Recovery, examines addiction and includes personal testimonies of teens who have gone through drug addiction and treatment. Chapter Five, Making Decisions About Drugs and Your Life, concludes this volume; its essays acknowledge that making decisions about drugs is something every individual teen must confront. It is hoped that the readings in this book will help people make informed decisions about drugs. With so much at stake, such decisions should not be made without careful consideration.

Chapter 1

The Lure of Drugs

Young People Talk About Drugs

Misti Snow

In 2000 the *Minneapolis Star-Tribune* solicited student essays on why young people use illegal drugs and alcohol for its Mindworks program, a monthly student forum. In the following article, *Star-Tribune* staff reporter Misti Snow examines the students' responses and concludes that there are a variety of reasons why some young people try drugs, including peer pressure, curiosity, and stress.

A sk almost any young person why some preteens and teens use illegal drugs and alcohol, and they'll reel off enough reasons to make any drug educator proud and any parent worried: depression, loneliness, peer pressure, thrills, escapism, popularity, rebellion, confusion, family problems, curiosity, fun. Most can just as readily recite some of the dangers: addiction, disease, arrest, death.

Yet large numbers of students continue to use illegal drugs and alcohol, routinely or occasionally, according to the nearly 8,000 responses to this month's [January 2001] Mindworks [a monthly section of the *Minneapolis Star-Tribune* featuring student writings on select topics].

Mindworks first asked young people why some students use

Reprinted, with permission, from "Kids Offer Sobering Look at Illegal Drug and Alcohol Use," by Misti Snow, *Minneapolis Star-Tribune*, January 8, 2001. Copyright © 2001 Star-Tribune.

illegal drugs and alcohol, and what adults can do to help prevent such use, in December 1988. While most of this year's themes remain similar to those of 1988, a few significant changes appeared:

Most students now include cigarette smoking as a form of drug use. A new term is common—"anti-drug"—used by those with a strong personal reason for not using drugs. And advertising and the entertainment media are more frequently named as major factors in luring teens to drugs.

In general, most elementary-aged students listed the well-known reasons given for drug use, such as peer pressure, popularity and depression. They vowed that they would never, ever use. Many of the fourth-through sixth-graders said they had received drug education, usually DARE (Drug Abuse Resistance Education) and they spoke highly of such programs and recommended that the programs continue through middle school and high school.

Sarah Graham, 10, of St. Paul, wrote "I know for a fact that some of the fifth- and sixth-graders will grow up to be drinkers and drug takers, but the DARE program most likely stopped many people from even thinking about doing drugs and drinking."

Pressure to Try Drugs

A reason why some of those students will go on to use is because as students age, pressure increases. Most commonly, the pressure to use begins at about middle school, although some students said their first encounters with drugs occurred when they were as young as 8. That exposure increases and is especially strong in high school, when parties become commonplace and kids are more rebellious.

> Many teens said the need to belong underlies the appeal of drug use.

Eighth-grader Rachel Rydel of Maplewood imagined the scene: "You're at a party. This is the best party you've been to. The music is pounding and the house is packed. All around you, your friends are dancing, laughing and having a great time. Suddenly there is a cheer. You begin to see beer cans appear in many people's hands. All of a sudden, a can is placed in your hands. You hold it uncertainly, and there is a flutter in your heart. . . . What do you say?"

Steve Kelley © 1996 San Diego Union-Tribune/Copley News Service. Used with permission.

Many teens said the need to belong underlies the appeal of drug use. High schooler Joe Felion of St. Paul wrote, "If you ask an adolescent what the most important thing to them is, the answer will probably not be family, school or religion. More often than not the answer will be friends. . . . It is no surprise that they will do anything to fit in."

Relieving Stress

Many said teens use drugs or alcohol to relieve stress. With the pressures of school, part-time jobs, extracurricular activities, broken families, failed relationships and demanding parents, "getting away" can be appealing.

Kevin Boyer, 16, of Brooklyn Park wrote, "The kids feel they need to forget their problems for a while and get high or drunk. Some people think if you do it, the problems in your life will go away. That's not true, but if you forget your problems for at least a little while, isn't that better than not forgetting your problems at all?"

> Easy accessibility [to drugs] is also a factor.

Some admitted that they use to get back at parents—parents who have divorced, parents who are too busy with work, overprotective parents who make every decision for their teens. Rachel Anderson, 12, of Richfield, wrote, "Teens and preteens don't get enough attention. These days some families don't even eat a meal together. The parents are so busy with work they don't have time for kids."

Easy accessibility is also a factor, said those who asserted that practically every teen in every town knows how to buy drugs. Often, said several, the suppliers are older siblings, older friends or even parents. A few said they know kids who smoke dope or drink with their moms or dads.

Scores of small-town and rural teens insisted that they use because there is nothing else to do. A 17-year-old girl from Madelia, Minn., wrote, "My parents drink when they are having fun. Since my parents are having fun doing it, then why can't I have fun and do it? Alcohol just makes a little boring town more exciting."

Parents Play a Key Role

Preventing teen drug use is complicated, but not impossible, said most. Parents are key to raising teens who either won't use or whose use will be minimal. Open communication is essential and both preteens and teens pleaded for parents to not lecture, not yell, not assume, but instead to talk calmly and to listen.

Some said that parents should institute curfews, chaperone parties, keep their own liquor locked up and know their children's friends. Parents also should be aware if their teens seem depressed.

Several said adults who supply teens with drugs should be severely punished; others wish for sophisticated technology that could detect fake IDs. Schools could have more locker searches, backpack searches and mandatory drug tests, said some. Perhaps more stress management courses for teens would be helpful, suggested one.

"One way to prevent drug and alcohol use is to stop advertising it to us," wrote eighth-grader Janessa Ide of Gaylord, Minn. "We see it everywhere in magazines, on TV and on billboards. No wonder so many kids do it. It's like they're telling us to."

Drug Education

Drug education is helpful, said most, but the most potent influence is hearing from other teens or adults who have had bad experiences when using drugs. Some said that simply watching their friends behave foolishly at parties and throw up afterwards is enough to curb their curiosity.

The lessons have come hard for those who have watched drug-abusing friends or siblings as their personalities change, grades plummet and dreams evaporate. Some have lost loved ones to addiction or drunken driving; a couple said they have brothers who are in jail for selling drugs.

Perhaps adults could better understand the teens' situation if they tried to answer these questions posed by Carissa Sloan, 13, of Maplewood:

"Can you remember the first time you tried drugs? What were you going through at the time? Chances are you experimented and can answer those questions. If you haven't, that's great, but what held you back from using?"

Why Teens Try Drugs

Melissa Krolewski

Why do teens try drugs? According to high school student journalist Melissa Krolewski, boredom, curiosity, and a desire for fun are all reasons given by teens she interviewed. However, for some teens, drugs become a trap as they seek to recapture or exceed the "high" they have gotten from drugs before. Krolewski was on the writing staff of *New Youth Connections,* a teen-written magazine in New York City.

These days, teens throughout New York take a variety of drugs—everything from the codeine in Mom's medicine cabinet to pot and angel dust. They inhale Whip-its and sniff cocaine, eat mushrooms and drop acid. A few do it for fun once in a while and still manage to accomplish some of their goals in life.

But others get carried away, lose their old friends, their ambition and even stop going to school. Some people lose more than that and find themselves out on the street with nothing at all, not even their dignity.

Most teens who use drugs start by smoking pot when they're in their early or midteens. But "pot after a while gets boring," said Christmass (not her real name), 18. . . .

"If you want to get that hype, you go on to something else," Christmass said. "I have friends that used to do pot and acid

Reprinted from "From Pot to Acid to Heroin . . . ," by Melissa Krolewski, *New Youth Connections*, May/June 1996, by permission of *New Youth Connections*. Copyright © 1996 by Youth Communication, 224 W. 29th St., 2nd Fl., New York, NY 10001.

only. Now they're cokeheads. That upsets me. These are people I've known all my life and to see them at a point where they can get hurt or lose their job and be out on the street scheming, trying to get money to support their habit—that makes me sad."

Even if they didn't all get seriously addicted, almost all of the teens I interviewed did go on to use other drugs. After he had been smoking pot for a while, Sean, 17, . . . said a friend brought some cocaine over to his house. "I wanted a new experience," he told me.

Getting "Higher"

Tommy, 18, . . . went from smoking pot to dropping acid about a year ago. He feels that "in a way" pot is a stepping stone to other drugs. You say to yourself, "I got this much high this time," he explained, "let me see if I can get higher."

But it's not like teens like Sean and Tommy actually sit down and contemplate whether or not they're going to do another drug. Usually the drug just comes to them and they're forced to make a decision right then and there. If you want to get "higher," the drug you do is the drug that is available at the time. In Sean's case that drug was cocaine; in Tommy's, it was acid.

"It was a boring day," said Tommy. "[There was] nothing to do [but] smoke a joint, listen to the radio. [My friend] Paul came over and said, 'Hey Tommy, I got two trips, you wanna try it?' . . . I was like, 'OK, I'll try anything once'."

> It's not like teens . . . sit down and contemplate whether or not they're going to do another drug.

Christmass popped her first tab of acid when she was 14—even before she ever smoked pot. She was just hanging out when "this guy asked us if we wanted it," Christmass told me. "He had a whole sheet, he gave it to us for free. It was a little tiny piece of paper, I didn't think it would have any effect on us."

When you take a tab of LSD, your perception of everything

changes. And you see things different than they really are. Objects seem to change in size, color and shape right before your eyes. You might see things "melt" like a candle, or you might see things that aren't really there: patterns moving on a plain white wall, for example.

Seeing God

The first time Tommy tripped, "I thought I saw a cloud in the shape of God," he said. "Everything just took on a happy look. Like a cartoon. Like it's drawn, not built."

Roach, 17, . . . described how he "figured out" how the ocean was created. "One day around nightfall, the sky got too heavy and it turned into a gigantic drop," Roach said. "Then when it crashed down to the earth, it became a gigantic ocean. It was cool, I saw it happen."

Roach loves acid because he says, "reality can be molded and shaped however you please." And he realized that "the world is bigger than I thought."

Tales from the Dark Side

Although it's possible to have fascinating experiences like these doing drugs, it's also extremely easy to get in over your head. Like a roll of the dice, you never know exactly how a drug like LSD will affect your mind—or your life. You can get paranoid and have a bad trip, spend all your money, put yourself in a dangerous situation, lose all your motivation, or become "slower" (in other words, "burnt").

"There is a dark side," said Roach, becoming serious. The first time he had a "bad trip" Roach thought he had turned into a robot. "I was stuck in robot form [and] couldn't get out," he said. "I felt like I couldn't control the LSD. I felt like I lost my mind."

He also said he felt that he had committed some "horrible crime" and somehow deserved to be punished for it (even though he hadn't done anything wrong). "I felt like I was going to be taken away and never see any of my friends again," he said.

Tommy agrees with Roach. You do feel "invincible," he said. "Then again it will bite you in the ass. A bad trip will make you feel like you're *not* on top of the world—paranoid, suicidal." With acid you always have to expect the unexpected.

Getting Carried Away

With other drugs you may know how the high is going to feel, but sometimes the very desire to get high can push you to extremes you never before imagined. From the first time Sean did a few lines of coke, "I f—kin' loved it," he said. "It was the best feeling I ever had. I felt like I was in a pinball machine. I was being knocked around at high speed. I felt invincible."

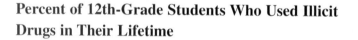

Percent of 12th-Grade Students Who Used Illicit Drugs in Their Lifetime

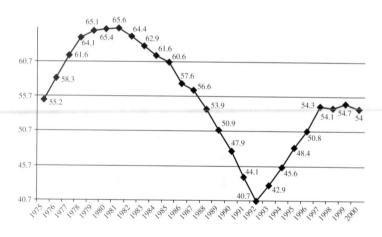

Monitoring the Future Survey, 2000, National Institute on Drug Abuse.

Before long, Sean was doing coke five days a week. "The only thing on my mind was coke," he said. "I was forgetting all of my other responsibilities and losing friends quick. I was only hanging out with those five people [who I did coke with]. I wasn't going to school." Fortunately, Sean was eventually able to see what was going on and decide that he didn't want to be involved with coke anymore.

But Paco Sanchez wasn't so lucky. Paco has taken every drug available to him—pot, heroin, coke, prescription pills, angel dust, Special K, acid, mushrooms, crystal meth, mescaline, crack, ecstasy, opium, hash and finally methadone. But now, at age 22, he regrets it.

> For many, drugs are part of growing up, but growing up means learning how to take responsibility for your own well-being.

Paco was taking the codeine he found in the medicine cabinet to get high when he was in the 6th grade. By the time he was 15, the codeine had stopped having an effect so Paco moved on to sniffing heroin. "Heroin felt just like codeine, but more intense," he said.

Crack Attack

When he was 19, Paco ran away to California, alone and with nothing but the clothes on his back. "I wanted to get high instead of staying with my parents," he said. In California, Paco had no friends and no place to go. He lived in the street, "experimented" with speed and got addicted to crack.

"I sold all my possessions, spent all my money and was homeless," he said. "I couldn't take a shower . . . I didn't care about [my] appearance. I just cared about crack. All day, every day. I was chasing tiny white rocks that make you feel good for just a few minutes."

After six months, Paco came back to New York. For a while he got himself into a drug program but the desire to get high was too strong. Paco got so carried away that he was sniffing heroin a few times a day. He'd used heroin before but this was the first time he'd been addicted to it.

"I wanted to stop, but I realized I couldn't," he said. When he tried, he suffered withdrawal pains: stomach cramps, hot and cold flashes, insomnia, sweats, fatigue and irritability. "I couldn't hold any food down," he added. ". . . It was like having the flu only 10 times worse."

Play It Smart

Today Paco is trying to turn his life around. He is in a program for recovering heroin addicts that gives him methadone, a drug that is supposed to help you gradually kick the habit. He lives in a one-room apartment with a close friend who cares about him, and he is desperately trying to get off methadone and find a job.

But it's hard. "Methadone is a b—ch to kick," Paco said. "I'm trapped because without my methadone, I can't live.

I wrote this story because I worry that too many teens are getting into things they don't know enough about. Like Paco, they are giving up their entire lives on an impulse. I know that being a teen means partying and having fun. But having fun doesn't have to mean being careless.

For many, drugs are part of growing up, but growing up means learning how to take responsibility for your own well-being. Don't ever let other people decide for you whether or not you want to do a particular drug. And if you do decide to try something, don't let yourself get to the point where you look back, like Paco, and say: "I feel like the past five years were a blur."

How Curiosity Led Me to Try Pot

Tamra Dawn

Widespread teen drug use is not a new phenomenon—it goes back to at least the 1960s. Tamra Dawn, a teenager during that decade, tells what happened to her when she tried smoking marijuana. Although her experiences with pot were generally positive, she advises teens today against experimenting with marijuana because of its legal and health risks. Dawn is now a mother of three and a correspondent for Wholefamily.com, an online family and teen advice website.

L ast week, I ran into one of my teenage nieces at a trance party. I was just there out of curiosity—really. "You are the coolest aunt," she told me.

She has a point. I've lived on a commune, hitchhiked across Europe, marched in demonstrations, have an open mind and love to experience new things.

It was that love of new things that led me to my first experience with pot, back in the '60s.

I was 18 and in my first year of college. My friend, Bill, and I went to his apartment to pick up the rest of our crowd, and a bunch of people were sitting around the table smoking a joint.

Do you want to try it? Bill asked.

Reprinted, with permission, from "Thoughts on Pot," by Tamra Dawn, online article at www.aboutteensnow.com/substance_abuse/drugs/pot.html. Copyright © 2000 WholeFamily Center, Inc.; www.wholefamily.com.

Sure, I said. I'm always up for an adventure. Besides, I knew some people who had smoked and nothing terrible had happened to them. And I trusted Bill.

So I sat there and inhaled and coughed—and coughed some more. I watched as one girl's eyes started turning red. Watched as she started laughing at everything anyone said. She looked like she was having a great time. I wanted to have a great time too, so I kept pulling the stuff into my lungs—but nothing happened.

The veterans told me that that often happens the first time.

The Second Time

The second time, I did it with my roommate, Shelly. We stuffed a towel into the crack of our dorm room door and lit up.

Wow. I think that's the highest I've ever been. After a few tokes, we started laughing and couldn't stop. I fell back on my bed and suddenly felt like I was on one of those stools that you can spin and it gets higher and higher. Only my stool was sitting on top of the planet and I was spinning off into outer space. Very weird.

We both felt it was more than we had bargained for, so we called our friend David in the dorm next door to help us through it. You'll know how high I was when I tell you that at some point, I was

> It was . . . love of new things that led me to my first experience with pot.

holding his hand and I looked down and thought that I was holding just a hand—unattached to a body. It was scary.

Over the next year or so, almost all my friends tried it. It was no big deal. We knew it was illegal and we were careful. We knew this one guy who got busted but he dealt. We weren't into that.

So I smoked off and on for a few years and then this funny thing started happening. Actually, I think it was happening all along, but it started to get to me. I would smoke and I would get kind of paranoid.

Like I remember this one time when I was with my boyfriend and my roommate. We had smoked and I had gone to the bathroom. I was looking in the mirror when I heard them laughing in the living room and I was sure they were laughing at me!

That kind of thing kept happening. I felt that marijuana frees up something inside you so that unconscious feelings swim up to the surface and you become aware of them. I was insecure to begin with, but usually managed to keep those feelings at bay. When I was high, I couldn't. There they were in all their glory—or I should say in all their difficulty and pain. I wasn't into feeling pain.

> I've . . . discovered other ways to get the benefits of pot without polluting my mind and body.

Later, I started to worry about stuff I'd heard about pot—like that it could affect your short-term memory. I didn't want that to happen to me. My father had lost his memory when he was old and I didn't want to take any chances with mine!

I kept hearing people say that you could get what I got from pot from regular meditation. And you know what—it's true. I've also discovered other ways to get the benefits of pot without polluting my mind and body. That same feeling washes over me when I wake up in the middle of the night with a new idea, when I'm in love, when I manage to plug into the universal creative energy that is both inside and around all of us—then I feel focussed, creative, tuned in—in short—high.

Three Reasons Not to Get High

So despite my early, mostly positive experiences, I would say: DON'T SMOKE MARIJUANA.

Three reasons:

One, just like alcohol, marijuana is something you should wait to do (if you do it at all) when you're an adult. It can lead you to all sorts of places that you just aren't ready to deal with. Also, I wouldn't want to take a chance with a body and brain that were still developing. They're the best things you've got and you don't want to risk screwing them up in any way.

Two, for some people it can be dangerous.

I have a very good friend who started smoking daily. It was just a few tokes, she said, to add color to her day. After a month or so, she got high and kind of didn't come down. She thought she was doing great: having lots of realizations, learning about herself, growing up all at once. She said she felt like she was having a growth spurt, like she had just gone through ten years of therapy in a week.

The problem was she was going too fast. During that last week, she hardly ate and barely slept. That Saturday, we had to take her to the emergency room. She started to say really weird things that no one could understand. She wasn't making sense. And we couldn't get through to her. At the hospital, they said she was having a "manic episode," gave her a shot of some kind of strong anti-psychotic drug and a day later she was back to normal. But she got a good scare. The doctor said it was probably the marijuana that did it. He told her it would be a good idea to never smoke again.

And three, depending on where you live, you could get into really big trouble with the law. I know of a girl whose sister got taken away to a foster home because their mother had given her money to buy pot. And the mother got charged with neglect. The sister's been in the foster home for months and the mom is fighting in the courts to get her back. That kind of thing can happen because marijuana is illegal.

One final thought. Although pot is one of the more "gentle" mind altering substances, it is still mind altering. And any time you are not in full control of yourself, you are not in the best shape to deal with things that come your way.

You want to be on top of the situation.

That's really the best way to be on top of the world.

My Experiences with LSD

Anonymous

Many people who try drugs do so seeking new experiences or sensations. In the following anonymously written account, a teenager tells of her experiences with LSD, one of the most commonly used hallucinogenic drugs. She explains that curiosity led her to sample the drug and describes the sometimes alarming results in her feelings and perceptions.

The names in this story have been changed.

Two years ago, I was a naive 14-year-old who didn't even know what acid was, nor had I ever in my wildest dreams imagined what effect it could have on my mind. Sure, I'd smoked pot plenty of times, but there's no comparison between weed and LSD. I wish I had known then what I know now.

Every Fourth of July my friends Angela and Judy and I go down to the river and watch the fireworks with our families. That year was special. Sam, a 20-year-old guy I had met in the park two days earlier, was going with us. Even though I had only known Sam a short time, I felt it had been years—an eternity. And even though I had no particular reason to, I trusted him.

Maybe that is why I smiled when, a couple of hours before the

Reprinted from "If You Trip, You Might Fall," by Anonymous, *New Youth Connections*, May/June 1996, by permission of *New Youth Connections*. Copyright © 1996 by Youth Communication, 224 W. 29th St., 2nd Fl., New York, NY 10001.

fireworks were supposed to start, he unfolded the shred of paper holding a half a tab of LSD and told me what it was. Sam said that if I slipped the tiny triangular piece of paper under my tongue, I would see fireworks even when I closed my eyes.

"What are you, nuts?" asked Judy when I hinted I might do it. "I wouldn't trust it if I were you," said Angela, plant-ing a double meaning. What they were actually saying was: "You don't even know the guy, and you're gonna trust him enough to take drugs with him?"

> I was determined to take the chance. I was curious.

I Was Curious

It was as if a higher power urged me on. (Then again maybe it was stupidity.) I was determined to take the chance. I was curi-ous: what did he mean, I'd see fireworks even when I closed my eyes? I opened my mouth and let him drop the supposedly miraculous piece of paper under my tongue.

After that we all went to a local park that was fenced off and had signs that said "No Trespassing." I showed Sam around. I was in a great mood. Leaving the park, we had to climb over an old gate. On my way over, I seemed to get stuck for a moment. I tugged on my leg, but it wouldn't budge. Then I glanced at everyone else, their mouths opened in horror. Looking back at my leg, I realized I had caught it on razor wire. A jagged piece of metal was stuck in me, but I felt no pain.

Feeling No Pain

I didn't know what to think, mainly because I had no idea what was going on. Was blood really rushing out of my leg? Judy and Angela stood there speechless. Sam told me that it was just a small cut and that I shouldn't look at it.

I was feeling no pain at all, not even when he bent down and pulled out the silver blade that was still lodged there. I just giggled, thinking the whole incident was hysterical. Sam insisted that I still not look at it, even though it was such a tiny cut. "It's mind over matter," he told me.

The four of us walked to Angela's house, where our parents were waiting for us. Nothing was too out of the ordinary. I just felt extra happy. "Not a bad drug," I thought. When we reached Angela's, the parents were sitting at the dining room table, talking and drinking coffee. I introduced Sam and we watched TV for a while.

Concrete Waves, Wiggling Lampposts

It was about 8 P.M. Outside you could hear music blasting, the rumble of fireworks, and occasionally loud laughter. Sam and I went outside to enjoy all the racket. We walked down the block and smoked a joint. From then on, things began to change.

Judy and Angela weren't with us and I remember thinking I should go upstairs and ask them to come outside. I missed them. But I was getting more and more confused. It was like I had forgotten how to go upstairs. So I just sat on the steps and watched the pretty colors flying through the air, wondering how much money the neighbors had spent on fireworks.

I was in my glory. The night air was warm on my skin and Sam and I were getting to know each other. He asked me to be his girlfriend.

> The light posts began to wiggle like they were dancing.

Nine o'clock rolled around and we all started walking towards the river. Somewhere between the river and Angela's, things started to look strange. The pavement began to look as if it were part of the river; waves formed in the concrete as if the tide were coming in. The light posts began to wiggle like they were dancing. It was hard to believe that such a tiny piece of paper could do all this. I was finding it hard to even remember how to walk. The concrete tide was getting higher and higher. Was it going to swallow me?

I began to really freak out. I didn't know what normal was anymore, so I didn't know how I should act. My mind didn't feel right. I stopped talking, I figured that whatever came out of my mouth would be wrong, and everyone would know I was on some kind of drugs. Whenever someone talked to me, I just smiled and pretended I was having fun.

Percentage of U.S. Twelfth Graders Reporting That It Is "Fairly Easy" or "Very Easy" to Get Marijuana, LSD, or Ecstasy, 1989–1999

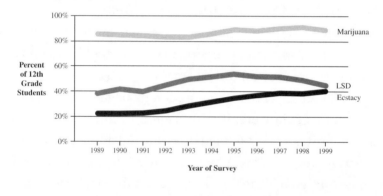

Center for Substance Abuse Research (CESAR), September 18, 2000.

When we all got to the river, the crowd was unbearable. I remember looking at Judy and Sam, and somehow they had exchanged eyes. Judy had Sam's eyes and Sam had Judy's. At that point I felt like I was going insane and I would never be the same.

My mother asked me if I wanted ice cream and I kept saying "What?" She started yelling at me, saying that I was embarrassed to eat ice cream in front of Sam. Something in my brain snapped at that moment and wouldn't allow me to comprehend what anyone was saying. I felt trapped.

Everything Sounded Like Jibberish

We never got to see the fireworks. It seemed that we had arrived too late. We all headed toward the park, my mother giving Sam the third degree. "What's going on?" I kept asking myself. I knew my mom was angry, but I couldn't understand why. I couldn't even stick up for Sam because I didn't know what my mother was saying. It sounded as if everyone was talking another language—jibberish.

My mom was screaming at the top of her lungs now. Poor Sam, I was surprised he didn't just walk away. It seemed as if Sam started chanting "run with me, run with me." I took a last look at my hostile mother and, well, ran with him.

We walked for a while. I felt like I had just escaped from a mental hospital. Sam and I sat down by some factories. My nerves were like a set of electrical wires during a rainstorm.

"Trust Me"

"Relax and enjoy it," Sam said and smiled. I felt like he was my guardian angel. I was comprehending everything now, my "peak" was over. Then I heard my mother's voice calling my name. "She's here," I thought. I was staring at a garbage can. I told Sam and he said, "Trust me, your mom's not here. It's OK." He said "trust me" a million times and I finally gave in.

I calmed down and closed my eyes. I did see the fireworks that I had missed at the river. Sam and I talked on and on into the night. There was some kind of magic bond between us. I felt strangely safe with him. Thank God, because otherwise I think I would have literally been going crazy.

> Now that I am more aware of the dangers, I'm still not sure if I will ever do it again.

About 4 A.M., we decided to say goodnight. I wondered when I'd see Sam again. It had been one nutty night. I walked through the streets full of dead fireworks and liquor bottles. When I got home, my mom apologized for embarrassing the hell out of me. Then she asked what had happened to my leg.

I looked down and suddenly realized that the "tiny" cut was

really a huge gash. The blood actually glued my stockings onto me. And it didn't even hurt. Jeez, I guess I was really high at the time, and I didn't even know it.

The Day After

The next day, I remember feeling depressed, probably because the world was amazingly colorful and new when I was on the LSD and now it was back to the same old, dull world I knew before.

Looking back, I am still glad that I tried LSD, however, because it was an amazing experience. My first acid trip enabled me to see beyond reality and made me more open-minded in some ways. But I also know now just how dangerous it can be. I wish that I had understood the effects of acid before I did it, that way maybe I would have been better prepared.

I now know that you shouldn't just take acid from anyone. Only God knows what it'll do to you and your body. I found out the hard way that tripping with my mom around is a no-no, for example. And, if you're not comfortable where you are and who you're with, you are very likely to get paranoid and have a bad trip.

I also realize now that I freaked out because I thought it was me who was strange, when it was only the LSD. At the time, I didn't know it would go away in eight hours.

I still have a scar on my leg from that first acid trip and just thinking about it terrifies me. Something much, much worse could have happened to me. Even trusting Sam was incredibly dumb. He could've turned out to be a maniac and hurt me. Sam could have even left me alone, which would have been so frightening I might have really gone insane. My mind was so messed up back then that whatever he told me, I would have believed. You know the saying, "If he jumped off a roof, would you jump too?" Well, on LSD I most likely would have.

Basically, I went into it blindly and that is the worst thing I could have done to myself. I've done acid a few more times after that because I wanted to enjoy it. When Sam and I were sitting by the factories, and I had finally relaxed, I felt like LSD promised to be amazing. But when I tried it again I didn't feel totally in control. I was scared something would go wrong and I wouldn't be able to handle it. The thought of losing control scares me to the point where I can't have fun. If only acid wasn't so intense.

Now that I am more aware of the dangers, I'm still not sure if I will ever do it again. I'm at the point where I don't know whether or not it is really worth putting myself in such a dangerous situation.

Teens and Psychoactive Medications

Stephen Fried

Recent years have been marked by a growing awareness of the problem of mental illness—as well as a growing number of teens who are introduced to brain-altering drugs through prescribed medications such as Ritalin. Many people are beginning to analyze illegal drug use by teens in light of these two facts, argues Stephen Fried. Not only are children exposed early on to the idea of using drugs to solve their problems, but many are also experimenting with combinations of illegal and prescription drugs. Fried is the author of *Bitter Pills: Inside the Hazardous World of Legal Drugs.*

Michael had been taking Ritalin on school days since third grade, when he was first diagnosed with attention-deficit disorder, a learning disability. He thought it was probably an accurate diagnosis, even though he wondered why he hadn't been sent for evaluation until his parents got divorced. But only when he got to boarding school was he educated in the uses and broadening abuses of the pharmacopeia of legal and illegal drugs available to adolescents today.

At school, for instance, he learned the ABC's of mixing medi-

Excerpted from "Sex, Meds, and Teens," by Stephen Fried, *Rolling Stone*, May 11, 2000. Copyright © 2000 by Stephen Fried. Reprinted by permission of the author; www.stephenfried.com.

cine and alcohol. "If you're drinking and on Ritalin, it probably doubles or triples the alcohol effect," he explains almost clinically. "When you're on an anti-depressant, it does the same thing, but it knocks you out. You know, it says so right on the bottle.". . .

The childproof cap is off the pill bottle. Prescribing medications to kids as freely and haphazardly as to adults is no longer taboo. And a New Drug Culture has emerged, the legal one most familiar to kids today. This is the first generation ever to practice chemical manipulation of the brain with parent-approved medications long before being exposed to the standard illegal recreational substances.

And we've moved far beyond Ritalin, which is still one of the few psychoactive medications specifically approved for use in patients under eighteen. Today, drug companies are in the home stretch of the race to get Food and Drug Administration approval to market Prozac and other anti-depressants directly to kids— possibly even through TV ads.

When Prozac was approved for adult use in the late 1980s, it changed the way Americans felt about the use of psychiatric medicines. The same thing is likely to happen when the drug is approved for patients under eighteen. And kids being treated for serious mental illnesses will increasingly be joined by young patients who aren't that sick, or might not be sick at all. But teens will still be asked to try some of the most powerful and expensive psychiatric drugs available—in part because the HMO-driven treatment market often views pills as more cost-effective than therapy or counseling. . . .

It's important to note that many of the new and newly prescribed psychoactive medications will save young lives: According to Dr. Kay Redfield Jamison's recent book, *Night Falls Fast,* depression leading to suicide kills more teenagers and young adults than cancer, heart disease, AIDS, pneumonia, influenza, birth defects and stroke combined.

But the new drug culture is being driven by more than symptoms. Perhaps more powerful are the new market forces. Psychoactive medication has been possibly the single most promising growth area in the pharmaceutical industry—in terms both of medicinal innovation and sales volume. And patients under eighteen are now among the largest target growth markets for psychoactive drugs. . . .

Mixing Legal and Illegal Drugs

And as the thirteen-year-old who is taking anti-depressants, stimulants or anti-psychotics—or all three—becomes the regular kid rather than the oddball, the new drug culture is slamming head-first into the old one. Kids are prolifically mixing legal and illegal drugs. For years, medical journals have published occasional case studies of such situations; in March 2000, the front page of the *New York Times* carried the story of the Trinity College senior who died after he and three other students took Xanax, Valium, butalbital and sleeping pills—and possibly heroin.

In 1999, the National Institute on Drug Abuse (NIDA) released the first major study to determine whether early use of Ritalin makes kids more likely to try illegal drugs as teens. The study said no, but it did little to undermine the widespread suspicion that early medication use must have an impact on how teenagers view recreational drug play. Michael, for example, believes that "the more familiar you are with drugs at a younger age, the more you think they are part of everyday life—and that humans need drugs to deal with reality. At least, that's the way it was for me."

Experts used to think that most drug abuse grew out of "normal" kids "experimenting" and "getting hooked." NIDA director Dr. Alan I. Leshner explains that clinicians thought that only a small population of kids illegally used psychoactive drugs because they suffered from clinical depression, mania or some other mental illness—and were "self-medicating."

> A New Drug Culture has emerged.

Now Leshner thinks the opposite might be true, and of the 2 million kids under eighteen who use illegal drugs, a substantial number may be self-medicating for mental illness.

"Ten years ago," he says, "nobody believed there was such a thing as child and adolescent mental disorders. It's almost as if people didn't take what kids were feeling seriously. We figured, 'You'll grow out of it.' Ten years ago, nobody thought there was childhood schizophrenia. Kids were just weird.

"Now we believe there are 8 to 10 million kids with untreated mental illness," he says. But he concedes that the medical system's approach to prescribing for patients under eighteen still isn't ideal. "I help run a clinic at Yale, and in my private practice I see children," he says. "Many of these kids have tried medicines they thought would work that didn't. Many haven't been monitored adequately. Some were misdiagnosed in the fifteen minutes a doctor has to see a kid. It's fair to ask how well these medications are being used. It's not something the prescribers take lightly. But some drugs certainly are being prescribed without proper evaluation. And a lot of kids who need drugs don't get them."

A Fine Line

Sandy is a teacher at a large suburban high school that runs a special program for teenagers with psychiatric histories. There are few programs like it in the country, which is why Sandy asks that no further identifying details be given—her classroom is already overflowing. Before this job, Sandy worked at a large, old psychiatric hospital where analysis was still practiced and older psychiatrists shared the traditional reluctance to medicate children. So she has seen the new drug culture grow up right before her eyes. She has mixed feelings.

"The problem is that behaviors considered normal in adolescents would be pathology in adults," she says. "And medication has come to be seen as one way of controlling aberrant behavior. There are some behaviors which are so destructive and cannot be controlled in any other way: It's better to control them with medication than to lock the person up. On the other hand, one of the biggest issues I hear from kids is that medication changes who they are as people. They get very angry about that and resentful of people imposing their values on them."

Sandy hears from her kids about the fine line between legal and illegal drug use. "There's a strong feeling of the hypocrisy of a society that can so easily prescribe so many of these mind-altering medications and still have so much trouble with illegally defined drugs—especially marijuana," she says. "I hear a lot of, 'How come I can go to the doctor to relax when I could just smoke a joint and relax?'"

Katie's Story

Sandy suggests that I speak with Katie, a former student who has been on various psychoactive medicines since the ninth grade. Katie is now a college freshman and is sometimes amazed at people's casual attitudes about the world of meds. "You have the mini pill book in your bedroom somewhere—everybody has one," she jokes. "You know what every pill does, and if somebody has something new that nobody else has tried, the 'therapy kids' will all talk about it."

It hasn't always been this way. Katie's first years of treatment were torturous. "In ninth grade I was lethargic, crying a lot—the normal things a teenage girl would go through," she says. "Didn't like going to classes, got anxious all the time. So my mom sent me to a psychiatrist, who tried a lot of different things and then started me on Prozac.

"Taking Prozac was hard because of the way people talk about it. I kinda resent the name Prozac, because of all those articles about 'Why are we medicating our children?' and family values. The message is, 'You're weak; you have to take something unnatural; your brain works right if you'd let it.' When I read a magazine, I feel belittled."

During much of her experience with psychiatric meds, Katie was also smoking pot. "A lot of people self-medicate with marijuana because they don't want to take their pills," she explains.

Kids are prolifically mixing legal and illegal drugs.

"Maybe you don't trust authority, or you know you could sell your pills to get other drugs. I remember in high school, if you had your wisdom teeth out, people would say, 'Want to give me your Percocet?' I finally stopped smoking marijuana and mixing it with meds because I had a really bad night. I smoked a lot of pot, and I snorted some Ritalin. I had a panic attack. I was hallucinating. I felt there was a helmet going over my head and when the helmet got over my chin, I would die. Finally, I threw up."

Katie has no doubt that psychoactive drug therapy has saved her life many times over. Yet it's significant how her ambivalence about what she is doing still tugs at her.

"I talk to people who have depression and won't take medication," she says, "and it's hard for me to converse with them after they say they just stopped taking it. They go into their little speeches about the evils of medicating yourself with things that aren't natural. Yet sometimes I think they're right."

Katie does understand that in the new drug culture, medicine and metaphor can never be separated completely. "It's more acceptable in my generation to take medications, but my generation also wants to get riled up," she says. "I don't think a lot of people want to take medications. They don't want to trust authority, because they want to have a cause."

To her, the war of words over kids on psychoactive meds is "our Vietnam. Medication is a symbol of authority, of being controlled by something that isn't your own emotions. We don't want adults telling us to take this. We don't want to make things easier for adults by taking these meds."

Chapter 2

Some Facts

About Drugs

Teen

Decisions

Questions and Answers About Marijuana

National Institute on Drug Abuse

The National Institute on Drug Abuse (NIDA), part of the U.S. Department of Health and Human Services, conducts research on drug abuse in order to improve addiction prevention and treatment programs. Its brochure *Marijuana: Facts for Teens,* featured here, addresses questions many teens may have about marijuana. Among the points NIDA covers are the effects of marijuana on the body, the brain, and human behavior.

Q: *What is marijuana? Aren't there different kinds?*

A: Marijuana is a green, brown, or gray mixture of dried, shredded leaves, stems, seeds, and flowers of the hemp plant. You may hear marijuana called by street names such as pot, herb, weed, grass, boom, Mary Jane, gangster, or chronic. There are more than 200 slang terms for marijuana.

Sinsemilla (sin-seh-me-yah; it's a Spanish word), hashish ("hash" for short), and hash oil are stronger forms of marijuana.

All forms of marijuana are mind-altering. In other words, they change how the brain works. They all contain THC (delta-9-tetrahydrocannabinol), the main active chemical in marijuana. They also contain more than 400 other chemicals. Marijuana's

Reprinted from the National Institute on Drug Abuse's brochure *Marijuana: Facts for Teens,* November 1998, available at www.nida.nih.gov/MarijBroch/MarijTeenstxt.html.

effects on the user depend on the strength or potency of the THC it contains. THC potency of marijuana has increased since the 1970s but has been about the same since the mid-1980s.

Q: How is marijuana used?

A: Marijuana is usually smoked as a cigarette (called a joint or a nail) or in a pipe or a bong.

Recently, it has appeared in cigars called blunts.

Q: How long does marijuana stay in the user's body?

A: THC in marijuana is strongly absorbed by fatty tissues in various organs. Generally, traces (metabolites) of THC can be detected by standard urine testing methods several days after a smoking session. However, in heavy chronic users, traces can sometimes be detected for weeks after they have stopped using marijuana.

Most Teens Abstain

Q: How many teens smoke marijuana?

A: Contrary to popular belief most teenagers have not used marijuana and never will. Among students surveyed in a yearly national survey, only about one in five 10th graders report they are current marijuana users (that is, used marijuana within the past month). Fewer than one in four high school seniors is a current marijuana user.

Q: Why do young people use marijuana?

A: There are many reasons why some children and young teens start smoking marijuana. Most young people smoke marijuana because their friends or brothers and sisters use marijuana and pressure them to try it. Some young people use it because they see older people in the family using it.

> All forms of marijuana are mind-altering.

Others may think it's cool to use marijuana because they hear songs about it and see it on TV and in movies. Some teens may feel they need marijuana and other drugs to help them escape from problems at home, at school, or with friends.

No matter how many shirts and caps you see printed with the marijuana leaf, or how many groups sing about it, remember this: *You don't have to use marijuana just because you think everybody else is doing it. Most teens do not use marijuana!*

Marijuana's Effects

Q: What happens if you smoke marijuana?

A: The effects of the drug on each person depend on the user's experience, *as well as:*

- how strong the marijuana is (how much THC it has);
- what the user expects to happen;
- where (the place) the drug is used;
- how it is taken; and
- whether the user is drinking alcohol or using other drugs.

Some people feel nothing at all when they smoke marijuana. Others may feel relaxed or high. Sometimes marijuana makes users feel thirsty and very hungry—an effect called "the munchies."

Some users can get bad effects from marijuana. They may suffer sudden feelings of anxiety and have paranoid thoughts. This is more likely to happen when a more potent variety of marijuana is used.

Q: What are the short-term effects of marijuana use?

A: The short-term effects of marijuana include:

- problems with memory and learning;
- distorted perception (sights, sounds, time, touch);
- trouble with thinking and problem-solving;
- loss of coordination; and
- increased heart rate, anxiety.

These effects are even greater when other drugs are mixed with the marijuana—and users do not always know what drugs are given to them.

Q: Does marijuana affect school, sports, or other activities?

A: It can. Marijuana affects memory, judgment and perception. The drug can make you mess up in school, in sports or
clubs, or with your friends. If you're high on marijuana, you are
more likely to make stupid mistakes that could embarrass or
even hurt you. If you use marijuana a lot, you could start to lose
interest in how you look and how you're getting along at school
or work.

Athletes could find their performance is off; timing, move-
ments, and coordination are all affected by THC. Also, since
marijuana use can affect thinking and judgment, users can forget to have safe sex and possibly expose themselves to HIV, the
virus that causes AIDS.

**Percentage of U.S. Teens Reporting Use of Marijuana
in Last Twelve Months**

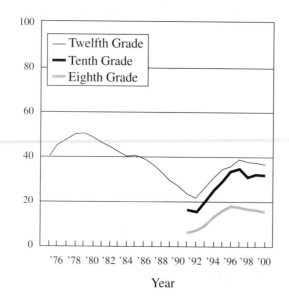

Monitoring the Future Study, University of Michigan, 2000.

Q: What are the long-term effects of marijuana use?
A: Findings so far show that regular use of marijuana or THC
may play a role in some kinds of cancer and in problems with

the respiratory, immune, and reproductive systems.

- *Cancer.* It's hard to know for sure whether regular marijuana use causes cancer. But it is known that marijuana contains some of the same, and sometimes even more, of the cancer-causing chemicals found in tobacco smoke. Studies show that someone who smokes five joints per week may be taking in as many cancer-causing chemicals as someone who smokes a full pack of cigarettes every day.

- *Lungs and airways.* People who smoke marijuana often develop the same kinds of breathing problems that cigarette smokers have: coughing and wheezing. They tend to have more chest colds than nonusers. They are also at greater risk of getting lung infections like pneumonia.

- *Immune system.* Animal studies have found that THC can damage the cells and tissues in the body that help protect people from disease. When the immune cells are weakened, you are more likely to get sick.

Other Questions

Q: Does marijuana lead to the use of other drugs?

A: It could. Long-term studies of high school students and their patterns of drug use show that very few young people use other illegal drugs without first trying marijuana. For example, the risk of using cocaine is 104 times greater for those who have tried marijuana than for those who have never tried it. Using marijuana puts children and teens in contact with people who are users and sellers of other drugs. So there is more of a risk that a marijuana user will be exposed to and urged to try more drugs.

> Contrary to popular belief most teenagers have not used marijuana.

To better determine this risk, scientists are examining the possibility that long-term marijuana use may create changes in the brain that make a person more at risk of becoming addicted to other drugs, such as alcohol or cocaine. While not all young people who use marijuana go on to use other drugs, further research is needed to predict who will be at greatest risk.

Q: How can you tell if someone has been using marijuana?

A: If someone is high on marijuana, he or she might:

• seem dizzy and have trouble walking;

• seem silly and giggly for no reason;

• have very red, bloodshot eyes; and

• have a hard time remembering things that just happened.

When the early effects fade, over a few hours, the user can become very sleepy.

Q: Is marijuana sometimes used as a medicine?

A: There has been much talk about the possible medical use of marijuana. Under U.S. law since 1970, marijuana has been a Schedule I controlled substance. This means that the drug, at least in its smoked form, has no commonly accepted medical use.

THC, the active chemical in marijuana, is manufactured into a pill available by prescription that can be used to treat the nausea and vomiting that occur with certain cancer treatments and to help AIDS patients eat more to keep up their weight. According to scientists, more research needs to be done on marijuana's side effects and potential benefits before it is used medically with any regularity.

Q: How does marijuana affect driving?

A: Marijuana has serious harmful effects on the skills required to drive safely: alertness, the ability to concentrate, coordination, and the ability to react quickly. These effects can last up to 24 hours after smoking marijuana. Marijuana use can make it difficult to judge distances and react to signals and sounds on the road.

> Marijuana affects memory, judgment and perception.

Marijuana may play a role in car accidents. In one study conducted in Memphis, TN, researchers found that, of 150 reckless drivers who were tested for drugs at the arrest scene, 33 percent tested positive for marijuana, and 12 percent tested positive for both marijuana and cocaine. Data have also shown that while smoking marijuana, people show the same lack of coordination on standard "drunk driver" tests as do people who have had too much to drink.

> Regular use of marijuana . . . may play a role in some kinds of cancer.

Q: *If a woman is pregnant and smokes marijuana, will it hurt the baby?*

A: Doctors advise pregnant women not to use any drugs because they could harm the growing fetus. One animal study has linked marijuana use to loss of the fetus very early in pregnancy.

Some scientific studies have found that babies born to marijuana users were shorter, weighed less, and had smaller head sizes than those born to mothers who did not use the drug. Smaller babies are more likely to develop health problems. There are also research data showing nervous system problems in children of mothers who smoked marijuana.

Researchers are not certain whether a newborn baby's health problems, if they are caused by marijuana, will continue as the child grows. Preliminary research shows that children born to mothers who used marijuana regularly during pregnancy may have trouble concentrating.

Marijuana and Addiction

Q: *What does marijuana do to the brain?*

A: Some studies show that when people have smoked large amounts of marijuana for years, the drug takes its toll on mental functions. Heavy or daily use of marijuana affects the parts of the brain that control memory, attention, and learning. A working short-term memory is needed to learn and perform tasks that call for more than one or two steps.

Smoking marijuana causes some changes in the brain that are like those caused by cocaine, heroin, and alcohol. Some researchers believe that these changes may put a person more at risk of becoming addicted to other drugs, such as cocaine or heroin. Scientists are still learning about the many ways that marijuana could affect the brain.

Q: Can people become addicted to marijuana?

A: Yes. While not everyone who uses marijuana becomes addicted, when a user begins to seek out and take the drug compulsively, that person is said to be dependent or addicted to the drug. In 1995, 165,000 people entering drug treatment programs reported marijuana as their primary drug of abuse, showing they need help to stop using the drug.

According to one study, marijuana use by teenagers who have prior serious antisocial problems can quickly lead to dependence on the drug.

Some frequent, heavy users of marijuana develop a tolerance for it. "Tolerance" means that the user needs larger doses of the drug to get the same desired results that he or she used to get from smaller amounts.

Q: What if a person wants to quit using the drug?

A: Up until a few years ago, it was hard to find treatment programs specifically for marijuana users.

Now researchers are testing different ways to help marijuana users abstain from drug use. There are currently no medications for treating marijuana addiction. Treatment programs focus on counseling and group support systems. There are also a number of programs designed especially to help teenagers who are abusers. Family doctors are also a good source for information and help in dealing with adolescent marijuana problems.

The Dangers of Ecstasy and Other "Club Drugs"

Sean O'Sullivan

Many people, including some teens, use recreational drugs at nightclubs or at all-night dance parties called "raves." These so-called club drugs include MDMA ("Ecstasy"), ketamine, and GHB. Freelance writer Sean O'Sullivan provides a brief summary of what these drugs are, how they are taken, and how they affect the human brain and body. He also examines other drugs that are commonly abused at clubs, including methamphetamine and cocaine.

The list of club drugs available these days can sound like a convoluted alphabet soup. There's X and XTC for Ecstasy, K, GHB, and LSD, just to name a few. Before you pop them in your mouth, under your tongue, or up your nose, though, you should know that a lot of these drugs are still being studied for their long-term effects. The more you know about the effects they can have on the body and on brain chemistry, the easier it might be to decide whether the risks outweigh the high.

The studies on the numbers of people taking club drugs are still surfacing. In 1997, 6.9 percent of 12th graders, 5.7 percent of 10th graders, and 3.2 percent of 8th graders reported that they had used Ecstasy/MDMA at least once in their lives. In 1998,

Excerpted from "Club Drugs," by Sean O'Sullivan, online article at www.drdrew. com/publish/healthwise/A172.html. Copyright © 1999 by drDrew.com. Reprinted with permission.

369,000 people ages 12 to 17 had done Ecstasy at least once in their life—about 1.4 percent of that age group, according to the National Household Survey on Drug Abuse. More than 1.4 million people ages 18 to 25 had taken Ecstasy at least once.

Long-Term Effects

Of course, the experts would say that any percentage is still too many people taking a drug they know so little about aside from its euphoric effects. The long-term damage Ecstasy can do is just beginning to be understood, according to Alan I. Leshner, Ph.D., director of the National Institute on Drug Abuse (NIDA). Even less is known about the effects on brain chemistry of drugs like ketamine ("Special K") and GHB ("liquid Ecstasy").

"Over time, Ecstasy is destructive to both dopamine and serotonin receptors. The neurons that respond to it are damaged," said Dr. Leshner. "These systems are involved in mood, pain and sleep. In primate studies, there is some data that even small amounts [of Ecstasy] cause permanent damage."

The problem is that the effects of this damage may not appear until years after the drug is taken. Dr. Leshner agrees that one of the more frightening aspects of club drugs, particularly when they are taken together, is that the people taking them are essentially volunteering as guinea pigs in an unofficial drug trial. "We are learning far too much from people's life experience with these drugs," he said. "It's very dangerous."

> The long-term damage Ecstasy can do is just beginning to be understood.

Nationwide statistics on deaths and emergency department admissions for drugs like Ecstasy are scarce and unreliable in the US. In Great Britain, where raves have long been on the official radar screen, Ecstasy has been linked to nearly 60 deaths since 1983 in a country where authorities estimate there are between 80,000 to 1 million or more regular users.

The important thing to realize is that "recreational drugs" are chemicals. Some of these drugs are powerful chemical compounds being taken in doses or for reasons they were never intended. They will have an effect on your night out—one that may even seem positive at the time—but they could also have unknown lasting effects on your body, your mood and your brain chemistry. Below are a list of some of the more common club drugs and what is known about their effects.

Ecstasy

(Also called: X, XTC, Adam, Eve)

Ecstasy typically comes in a pill form, often with symbols imprinted on the pill to signify a "brand name." Recent brands in New York include Tinky Winky, Mitsubishi, X-Files, Versace. It can also come in powder or capsule form.

Technically, Ecstasy is the chemical compound MDMA, but what you actually get can be any one of a variety of related "designer" compounds or pills combining anything from [psychoactive] drugs like MDA or 2CB to vitamin B_{12} and caffeine.

Serotonin and dopamine are neurotransmitters, or chemical messengers, that transmit messages across the synapses, or gaps, between adjacent cells in the brain (and other parts of the body). In the central nervous system, serotonin helps regulate mood, memory, and appetite. Dopamine is essential to the functioning of the central nervous system. Among its many functions, it plays a major role in controlling movement and emotion-based behaviors.

Ecstasy affects the serotonin and dopamine receptors in the brain, causing extensive and permanent damage even with limited use.

Clinical research shows that MDMA's parent drug, MDA, destroys serotonin-producing neurons, which play a direct role in regulating aggression, mood, sexual activity, sleep, and sensitivity to pain. Studies indicate that such damage to these receptors might lead to Parkinson's-like symptoms. These include tremors, poor coordination and, in extreme cases, a form of paralysis.

Deaths associated with Ecstasy appear rare and most that occurred were brought on either by hyperthermia (overheating) and the complications that follow or, very rarely, through excessive water consumption which has led to acute water intoxication.

GHB

(Also called: Liquid Ecstasy, Somatomax, Scoop, Grievous Bodily Harm)

GHB (gamma-hydroxybutryate) is typically available as an odorless, colorless and nearly tasteless liquid, or more rarely as a powder or capsule. At small doses, GHB reduces social inhibitions similar to alcohol. Too much GHB can cause vomiting, drowsiness, dizziness and seizures. As with

> The important thing to realize is that "recreational drugs" are chemicals.

Rohypnol ("roofies," "the date rape drug") GHB has been associated with sexual assault because it tends to lower the user's inhibitions. GHB may also produce withdrawal effects, including insomnia, anxiety, tremors, and sweating. Excessive use can cause comas, tremors, difficulty breathing and seizures. This risk is increased if the drug is combined with methamphetamine.

Methamphetamine

(Also called: Speed, Chalk, Meth, Tina, Ice, Crystal, Glass)

Typically found as a powder or pill, methamphetamine is snorted or mixed with water and injected. In another form, methamphetamine hydrochloride, it appears as clear chunky crystals resembling ice, which can be inhaled by smoking. In this form, it is referred to as ice, crystal, or glass.

Methamphetamine is highly addictive and is associated with serious health conditions, including memory loss, aggression, psychotic behavior, and potential heart and brain damage. It appears to have a neurotoxic effect, damaging brain cells that contain dopamine and serotonin. Over time, methamphetamine appears to cause reduced levels of dopamine, which can result in symptoms like those of Parkinson's disease, a severe movement disorder.

Animal research going back more than 20 years shows that high doses of methamphetamine damage neuron cell-endings. Dopamine- and serotonin-containing neurons do not die after methamphetamine use, but their nerve endings ("terminals") are cut back and re-growth appears to be limited.

Methamphetamine increases the heart rate and blood pressure and can cause irreversible damage to blood vessels in the brain, producing strokes. Other effects of methamphetamine include respiratory problems, irregular heartbeats, and extreme anorexia.

Ketamine

(Also called: K, Special K)

Typically available as a powder, ketamine is commercially produced in liquid form for use as an animal tranquilizer and as an anesthetic. The liquid form is processed into a powder that resembles powder cocaine.

Very little is known about the side effects of ketamine, an animal tranquilizer not widely studied in humans. It can cause psychosis, paranoia and have severe effects on motor skills. According to the Drug Enforcement Administration Office of Diversion Control, with repeated daily exposure, users can develop tolerance and psychological dependence.

> Mixing cocaine and alcohol is particularly dangerous.

Cocaine

(Also called: Coke, C, Crack, and a host of localized street names)

Cocaine is typically available in a powder form that is inhaled or mixed with water and injected. The crystalized form, "crack," is smoked.

There are numerous medical complications associated with cocaine use. Some of the most frequent complications are cardiovascular, including disturbances in heart rhythm and heart attacks. It can also cause respiratory effects, such as chest pain and respiratory failure, and neurological effects, including strokes, seizure, and headaches.

Cocaine is a strong central nervous system stimulant that interferes with the reabsorption process of dopamine. Physical effects of cocaine use include constricted peripheral blood vessels, dilated pupils, and increased temperature, heart rate, and blood pressure. Scientific evidence suggests that the powerful neuropsychologic reinforcing property of cocaine is responsible for continued use, despite harmful physical and social consequences.

High doses of cocaine and/or prolonged use can trigger paranoia. Smoking crack cocaine can produce a particularly aggressive paranoid behavior in users. Cocaine-related deaths are often a result of cardiac arrest or seizures followed by respiratory arrest. In rare instances, sudden death can occur on the first use of cocaine or unexpectedly thereafter.

Mixing cocaine and alcohol is particularly dangerous and compounds the physical effects of each. Research has found that the human liver combines cocaine and alcohol and manufactures a third substance, cocaethylene, which intensifies cocaine's euphoric effects, while possibly increasing the risk of sudden death.

What Hallucinogens Can Do to Your Brain

Kathiann M. Kowalski

Hallucinogens are a class of drugs that can radically change a person's thoughts, perceptions, and moods. Some hallucinogens are found in nature, while others are artificially synthesized. Kathiann M. Kowalski examines some of the most commonly used hallucinogens, including LSD, and describes how they affect the human brain. She recounts the experiences of several teens who took hallucinogens and concludes that these drugs can pose significant dangers. Kowalski writes for the magazine *Current Health 2*.

"You've got to help me," Raphael said, grabbing the emergency room doctor's arm. "The leprechauns are everywhere."

Restraining the terrified teen took five people. The "friend" who'd dropped Raphael off in the hospital parking lot didn't stick around to tell anyone what he'd taken. Meanwhile, the boy's heart raced at more than 160 beats per minute. His skin was flushed and dry. Within minutes, he went into seizures.

Finally a doctor with special toxicology training connected Raphael's rantings about little people to the hallucinogen jim-

Reprinted, with permission, from "What Hallucinogens Can Do to Your Brain," by Kathiann M. Kowalski, *Current Health 2*®, April/May 2000. Copyright © 2000 and published by Weekly Reader Corporation. All rights reserved.

sonweed. With no time to spare, the ER team gave Raphael medicine that saved his life.

Raphael's immediate emergency is over for now, but chances are he may continue to use hallucinogens. For many young people, hallucinogens remain a repeated threat.

Trips: Distorted Reality

Hallucinogens are drugs that cause hallucinations—the perception of something that isn't there. Hallucinogens also cause changes in thought and mood. Oddly, most users are aware that what they sense isn't real, but is drug-induced.

Some hallucinogen experiences, or trips, produce weird illusions. One user claimed he saw hordes of jabbering creatures "juggling incandescent neon microworlds."

Intensified sensations, such as brighter colors or louder sounds, occur in other trips. Still other trips bring a distorted sense of space and time. Users may feel like they're floating outside their bodies.

Another odd effect of hallucinogens is synesthesia. In synesthesia, senses get "crosswired." Users think they can see sounds or smell colors.

The weirdness can turn into horror. Sara took the hallucinogen ketamine. Afterward, the 16-year-old thought everyone dancing on the floor with her was decapitated. The image was gruesome.

One LSD user saw a giant lizard chewing a woman's neck. The plain carpet beneath his feet seemed to be a blood-soaked sponge. Still other hallucinogen users have reported sensations of being probed by slimy fingers or pulled down by grasping tentacles.

> For many young people, hallucinogens remain a repeated threat.

Terror and panic from bad trips breed paranoia—the irrational fear that everyone is after you. One high school sophomore felt so afraid after taking LSD that he ran screaming through fields in rural Michigan. Another LSD user threatened to attack his friend with a knife.

Abuse of hallucinogens surged during the 1960s and 1970s. During the 1980s, hallucinogen use dropped, but then it rose again in the '90s. The 1999 Monitoring the Future Study by researchers at the University of Michigan surveyed teen drug use. It found that about 14 percent of 12th graders had used hallucinogens at some point. The dramatic rise in usage rates—over 46 percent since 1991—raises serious health issues.

Natural and Synthetic Varieties

More than 100 chemicals are known hallucinogens. Some, like the jimsonweed Raphael took, come from plants. Jimsonweed contains the drug atropine. Its name comes from colonial Jamestown, where settlers became very ill after mistakenly eating it in a salad.

Peyote cactus buttons contain the drug mescaline. So-called magic mushrooms contain psilocybin and psilocin. One type of morning glory seed also produces hallucinogens.

Hallucinogens come from animals too. Certain toads secrete bufotenine. Besides distorting reality, the chemical causes high blood pressure, rapid heartbeat, blurred vision, and cramped muscles.

More potent hallucinogens come from laboratories. Using extracts from rye fungus, Swiss chemist Albert Hoffman developed LSD (lysergic acid diethylamide) in 1938. Also called acid, LSD was reported to be used by 13 percent of the 12th graders in the University of Michigan study. Less than 0.001 gram of LSD produces extreme hallucinations. LSD takes effect within 30 minutes. It lasts about 12 hours.

Another chemist, Alexander Shulgin, developed STP, or DOM (2,5-dimethoxy-4-methylamphetamine). The drug is over 50 times more potent than mescaline.

Other synthetic hallucinogens include DMA (dimethyloxyamphetamine), MDA (methylenedioxyamphetamine), and DMT (dimethyltryptamine). DMT's effects peak within minutes and usually wear off within an hour.

PCP (phencyclidine) is highly unpredictable. Some users feel out of touch with their bodies and surroundings. Others get so revved up they become violent. Because PCP is also an anesthetic, it deadens users' sense of pain. PCP's nicknames include angel dust, rocket fuel, and ozone.

> Sara took the hallucinogen ketamine. [She] thought everyone dancing on the floor with her was decapitated.

The veterinary anesthetic ketamine is also called Special K, Kit Kat, green, and blind squid. Because it's chemically like PCP, ketamine has similar effects.

Then there are a host of "designer drugs." Some produce distorted sensations and have other effects too. MDMA (methylenedioxymethamphetamine), or Ecstasy, first became popular in the 1980s at all-night parties called raves. Besides producing out-of-body sensations, Ecstasy is a powerful stimulant. Overdoses have killed young people.

Mind-Altering Drugs

How do hallucinogens work? The answers lie inside the brain.

Neurotransmitters are naturally produced chemicals. They carry messages between different nerve cells. Specific parts of nerve cells, called receptors, respond to specific neurotransmitters. To bind at a receptor, a chemical must fit just right—like a tiny jigsaw puzzle.

Serotonin, or 5-HT, is one neurotransmitter. It plays a role in sleep, memory, learning, mood, and behavior. It also affects body temperature, cardiovascular function, hormone secretion, and possibly pain sensation.

Fourteen kinds of receptors respond to serotonin. But LSD and similar hallucinogens (called classical hallucinogens) bind to only one group of these receptors, called 5HT-2 receptors.

This selective binding to only some serotonin receptors seems to be what triggers the drugs' hallucinogenic effects.

Mind-altering drugs that aren't classified with LSD affect different receptors. PCP, for example, appears to interfere with receptors for the neurotransmitter glutamate. It may also affect receptor sites for dopamine. Dopamine is linked to feelings of pleasure.

Scientists know that hallucinogens stimulate particular receptors in the brain. Exactly how that produces different types of hallucinations, however, remains largely a mystery. "We don't know exactly what's going on," admits Robert Findling at University Hospitals in Cleveland, Ohio. "We believe that hallucinations are a result of abnormal brain activity. Different parts of the brain become activated when they shouldn't."

Messing Up Your Mind

No one can predict when a hallucinogen user will have a bad trip. Dosage, the specific drug, and the setting in which it's taken all affect the user's experience. The bottom line, however, is that hallucinogens are unpredictable. That unpredictability makes them dangerous.

There's no effective treatment for a bad trip. Only having the drug wear off will make imagined demons go away. Books and articles recommend trying to calm distressed users in a quiet, uncrowded spot. But friends who are high themselves can't be counted on for help.

> No one can predict when a hallucinogen user will have a bad trip.

Flashbacks are even scarier. A flashback is a relived experience from a hallucination. Both frequent users and one-time experimenters can find themselves on another trip when they least expect it, such as while a teen is driving a car or performing gymnastics.

Flashbacks can suddenly bring back feelings of terror and paranoia. One young woman's flashback was so intense that she jumped out the window in a high-rise apartment building. The flashback came six months after her single experience with LSD.

Some hallucinogen users have needed treatment for serious psychological problems, as well as for their drug abuse. In certain instances, hallucinogen abuse seems to "unmask" preexisting psychological problems. Instead of resolving the underlying problem, however, hallucinogens only complicate things and add the additional problems that come with drug abuse.

Different hallucinogenic drugs affect the brain's receptors in different ways, with varying effects. Users may think they need the drugs to escape the pressures of day-to-day living. Or, they may continue taking the drug because their whole group uses hallucinogens. Whatever the reason, continued use means ongoing risks from the drugs.

Users also develop a tolerance to hallucinogens over time. In other words, they need more of the drugs to get the same effects. Higher doses greatly increase the risks of a bad trip and troubling flashbacks.

Complicating matters even more is the fact that hallucinogen users often abuse other drugs too, especially marijuana. Those other drugs bring along all their own physical and psychological risks, including the danger of addiction.

Physical Side Effects

Hallucinogens don't just mess with the mind. They have physical effects too, such as dilated pupils, warm skin, and excessive sweating.

LSD, Ecstasy, and most other hallucinogens increase heart rate and blood pressure, which can lead to sleeplessness and tremors. Overdoses can result in convulsions, coma, and heart and lung failure.

Users in the throes of a bad trip may hurt themselves. Some commit suicide to escape the trip's terrors. One study from the *Journal of Pediatrics* reported that 20 percent of adolescent hallucinogen users knew someone who'd had a suicide attempt or accident because of the drugs.

Incoherent speech, impaired coordination, and decreased awareness of touch and pain go along with many hallucinogens. Users also experience feelings of detachment and invincibility. After someone spiked her drink with PCP, 22-year-old Naomi wandered across town in icy cold weather without a coat. Cars barely missed hitting Naomi as she wandered. Later, she pondered jumping off a bridge. Naomi recalled feeling certain that nothing bad could happen to her.

Drownings, burns, falls, and motor vehicle crashes bring thousands of hallucinogen users to hospital emergency rooms each year. Sadly, many don't survive their hallucinogen-induced injuries. Violent behavior associated with hallucinogens lands other users in jail.

> Different hallucinogenic drugs affect the brain's receptors in different ways, with varying effects.

Specific hallucinogens may have their own toxic effects. Peyote can cause nausea. Mushroom users run the risk that collectors mistakenly picked toxic toadstools instead.

Long-term effects are a separate issue. A 1999 study by researchers at Johns Hopkins University suggests that Ecstasy harms brain cells. The full implications of the findings are not yet known. Of course, pregnant women who use hallucinogens or any other drugs risk harming their unborn children.

Long-term effects aren't limited to specific diseases, however. Paralysis from an accident, a criminal record, and severe psychological problems can ruin a teen's life. "These are bad, dangerous drugs," stresses Dr. Findling. "These can profoundly alter the course of a [teen's] life for the worse."

In Your Right Mind

Advocates of hallucinogen use from the 1960s claimed that the drugs could help harness creativity. Hallucinogens, however, are merely temporary tricks that affect the mind. "You're tricking your mind to see things that aren't there," warns Dr. Findling. "You end up doing things that you're not supposed to."

Indeed, people who hallucinate without taking drugs aren't society's creative geniuses. They're people with serious psychological problems. They don't function normally and need professional help. "You wouldn't want to do that to yourself," says Dr. Findling.

Instead of "dropping out," choose to live your life in the real world. Set realistic goals for yourself, and work toward them. Get involved with friends and family. Do activities that are important to you. Avoid hallucinogens, alcohol, and other drugs too. Then you can stay in touch with all your thoughts and perceptions. There's no better way to stimulate your creative spirit.

Basic Facts About Inhalants

American Council on Drug Education

Inhalant abuse is a serious drug problem, especially for younger teens. Inhalants are breathable chemicals that can be found in many common household products, such as cleaning fluids, paint thinners, and hair sprays. The following article by the American Council on Drug Education (ACDE) provides information on types of inhalants and their effects, which are often serious and can sometimes be fatal. ACDE is a drug abuse education agency affiliated with the Phoenix House, a nonprofit substance abuse treatment organization.

Inhalants are drugs that produce a quick, temporary high; lightheadedness; and euphoria (good feeling) when their fumes or gases are breathed and absorbed into the body through the lungs. The high is sometimes compared to the sensation of being drunk. It tends to last only a short time, from a few minutes to about three-quarters of an hour. It may be followed by after-effects like those of an alcohol hangover, such as drowsiness, headache, or nausea, which last for an hour or two.

Compared with other recreational drugs, inhalants are readily

Excerpted from "Basic Facts About Drugs: Inhalants," by the American Council on Drug Education, online article at www.acde.org/common/Inhalant.htm. Reprinted by permission of Phoenix House.

available and relatively cheap. Many of them can be obtained legally, even by minors, for more than a thousand common household products can be used to get high. It is partly for this reason, and partly because they are mistakenly believed to be safer than other recreational drugs, that inhalants are especially popular among children and young adolescents.

The average age at which adolescents first try these drugs is 13, and one eighth grader in five has used them. Dangerous and potentially lethal in their own right, inhalants often also serve as a gateway to other, stronger drugs.

Three Types

There are three main types of inhalants:

Organic solvents are liquid compounds of carbon that have the power to break down, or dissolve, other carbon compounds. Organic solvents are also highly volatile; they readily evaporate from a liquid to a gas or aerosol, which can be inhaled.

Many common products are either based on organic solvents or contain high concentrations of them. They include gasoline, lighter fluid and butane lighter fuel, spray paint, paint thinners and removers, transparent glue, rubber-cement thinner, hair spray, nail polish remover, degreasers, and cleaning fluids. Organic solvents are the easiest inhalants to obtain and the most dangerous to abuse.

Nitrites are compounds of nitrogen and act mainly as vasodilators, causing the walls of blood vessels to relax so that the vessels enlarge, or dilate. They are used medically to relieve attacks of angina chest pain caused by insufficient blood flow in the vessels serving the heart. They also tend to depress the activity of the central nervous system, producing the giddiness and euphoria of a high.

> The average age at which adolescents first try these drugs is 13.

The most commonly abused are amyl nitrite and butyl nitrite.

Amyl nitrite is usually packaged in small, crushable glass or plastic capsules, known as poppers or snappers. Butyl nitrite often comes in a bottle or spray can and is sold as an air freshener under names such as Rush, Locker Room, or Jac-Aroma.

> Inhalants can be very dangerous, both in their immediate effects and their long-term consequences.

Nitrous oxide, commonly called laughing gas, was the first inhalant used for recreational purposes. Introduced as an anesthetic in the 1850's, this compound of nitrogen and oxygen is still used medicinally, particularly by dentists. It doesn't completely block pain, but it does alter the perception of pain, so that there is no distress. Nitrous oxide tends to produce a pleasant, dreamy state of consciousness, somewhere between waking and sleep.

For medical use, nitrous oxide is compressed and stored in metal tanks, to which a hose and inhalant mask are attached. The compressed gas is also used to make whipped cream. When packaged in small cartridges, called whippets, and enclosed in a container of cream, the gas mixes with the cream when the nozzle is depressed. . . .

How Do Inhalants Harm You?

Because the immediate after-effects are usually mild and last only a short time, many abusers believe that inhalants are essentially harmless. They are wrong. Inhalants can be very dangerous, both in their immediate effects and their long-term consequences.

During the high itself and the period of reaction afterward, physical coordination and mental judgment are impaired, much as they are by excessive drinking. Abusers often suffer falls and other accidents and cannot drive safely. They may engage in irresponsible or dangerous behavior, such as reckless violence.

Inhalants irritate the breathing passages, sometimes provoking severe coughing, painful inflammation, and nosebleeds.

Nitrite inhalants often cause intense facial flushing, feelings of severe weakness and dizziness, and heart palpitations.

Inhalants, particularly in heavy doses, may not produce a pleasant high but mental confusion, hallucinations, and delusions of persecution (paranoia) instead.

What to Do When Someone Is Huffing

- Remain calm and do not panic.
- Do not excite or argue with the abuser when they are under the influence, as they can become aggressive or violent.
- If the person is unconscious or not breathing, call for help. CPR should be administered until help arrives.
- If the person is conscious, keep him or her calm and in a well-ventilated room.
- Excitement or stimulation can cause hallucinations or violence.
- Activity or stress can cause heart problems which may lead to "Sudden Sniffing Death."
- Talk with other persons present or check the area for clues to what was used.
- Once the person is recovered, seek professional help for abuser: school nurse, counselor, physician, other health care worker.
- If use is suspected, adults should be frank but not accusatory in discussions with youth about potential inhalant use.

National Inhalant Prevention Coalition, 1997.

By depressing the central nervous system, inhalants may dangerously hinder the activity of the nerves that control breathing. The resulting respiratory depression may cause unconsciousness, coma, or even death. The danger is especially great if inhalants are taken along with other nervous-system depressants, such as alcohol or barbiturates (sleeping pills).

Inhaling for an extended time from a bag or balloon may cause a dangerous shortage of oxygen in the lungs. Like respiratory depression, oxygen deprivation (asphyxia) may lead to unconsciousness, coma, or death.

> Even first-time users run the risk of sudden sniffing death.

Even first-time users run the risk of sudden sniffing death (SSD). The mechanics are not well understood, but abusers may suffer fatal irregularity of heartbeat (arrhythmia) or complete heart arrest. The risk of SSD seems to be higher if the abuser engages in strenuous physical activity or is suddenly startled.

Long-Term Effects

Repeated use tends to produce increased tolerance to the drugs and larger doses are needed to achieve the same results. Heavy doses in turn increase the risk of permanent brain damage, with effects such as poor memory, extreme mood swings, tremors, and seizures. Heavy, continuous use also increases the risk of heart arrhythmia and respiratory depression.

Nitrite inhalants tend to raise the pressure of the fluid within the eyes. The raised pressure may eventually lead to glaucoma and blindness. Regular nitrite abuse may also cause severe, pounding headaches.

Organic solvents are the most dangerous of all inhalants. They are poisons that break down organic compounds of all kinds including those that make up living cells. Once absorbed into the body, they tend to concentrate in the liver and kidneys, where they are processed for disposal. Repeated, heavy abuse may cause fatal damage to these organs, as well as to the heart and nervous system.

Signs of Abuse

Certain signs suggest that a person may be abusing inhalants:

- A sweetish, chemical smell on the clothes or body

- Inflammation of the nostrils, frequent nosebleeds, or a rash around the nose and mouth
- Poor appetite and loss of weight
- Pale, bluish skin
- Watery, bloodshot eyes with dilated pupils
- Slow, slurred speech
- Clumsy, staggering gait, and drunken appearance

Heroin Abuse and Addiction

National Institute on Drug Abuse

Heroin is a powerful narcotic that can be injected, smoked, or inhaled. Some people fear this drug is making a comeback among teens. The following brief article gives some basic information on what heroin is and how it affects the body and brain. It was produced by the National Institute on Drug Abuse (NIDA), a federal government agency.

Heroin is an illegal, highly addictive drug. It is both the most abused and the most rapidly acting of the opiates. Heroin is processed from morphine, a naturally occurring substance extracted from the seed pod of certain varieties of poppy plants. It is typically sold as a white or brownish powder or as the black sticky substance known on the streets as "black tar heroin." Although purer heroin is becoming more common, most street heroin is "cut" with other drugs or with substances such as sugar, starch, powdered milk, or quinine. Street heroin can also be cut with strychnine or other poisons. Because heroin abusers do not know the actual strength of the drug or its true contents, they are at risk of overdose or death. Heroin also poses special problems because of the transmission of HIV and other diseases that can

Excerpted from "Heroin Abuse and Addiction," a 1997 research report from the National Institute on Drug Abuse (NIH Publication No. 97-4165) published at http://165.112.78.61/ResearchReports/Heroin/Heroin.html.

occur from sharing needles or other injection equipment.

Heroin is usually injected, sniffed/snorted, or smoked. Typically, a heroin abuser may inject up to four times a day. Intravenous injection provides the greatest intensity and most rapid onset of euphoria (7 to 8 seconds), while intramuscular injection produces a relatively slow onset of euphoria (5 to 8 minutes). When heroin is sniffed or smoked, peak effects are usually felt within 10 to 15 minutes. Although smoking and sniffing heroin do not produce a "rush" as quickly or as intensely as intravenous injection, National Institute on Drug Abuse (NIDA) researchers have confirmed that all three forms of heroin administration are addictive.

> Heroin abusers . . . are at risk of overdose or death.

Short- and Long-Term Effects of Heroin Use

Short-Term Effects

- "Rush"
- Depressed respiration
- Clouded mental functioning
- Nausea and vomiting
- Suppression of pain
- Spontaneous abortion

Long-Term Effects

- Addiction
- Infectious diseases (e.g., HIV/AIDS and hepatitis B and C)
- Collapsed veins
- Bacterial infections
- Abscesses
- Infection of heart lining and valves
- Arthritis and other rheumatologic problems

Focus Adolescent Services, 2000.

Injection continues to be the predominant method of heroin use among addicted users seeking treatment; however, researchers have observed a shift in heroin use patterns, from injection to sniffing and smoking. In fact, sniffing/snorting heroin is now a widely reported means of taking heroin among users admitted for drug treatment in Newark, Chicago, New York, and Detroit.

With the shift in heroin abuse patterns comes an even more diverse group of users. Older users (over 30) continue to be one of the largest user groups in most national data. *However, several sources indicate an increase in new, young users across the country who are being lured by inexpensive, high-purity heroin that can be sniffed or smoked instead of injected.* Heroin has also been appearing in more affluent communities.

Point of Contention: Is Marijuana a Gateway Drug?

Much disagreement exists within American society regarding the extent to which marijuana is a dangerous drug (especially compared with alcohol and nicotine, both of which are legal for adults). One area of dispute is whether marijuana use can lead to the use of other drugs such as cocaine. Supporters of the "gateway drug" hypothesis argue that teens and others who try pot are far more likely to become involved with (and addicted to) other drugs, and that this is one reason why children and teens should be strongly dissuaded from trying marijuana. But some people have questioned the link between marijuana use and the abuse of other drugs, arguing that such a connection has not been proved.

Whether marijuana is truly a gateway drug is debated in the following two articles. Joseph A. Califano, a former cabinet secretary of health, education and welfare, is president of the National Center on Addiction and Substance Abuse at Columbia University in New York. John P. Morgan is a physician and professor of pharmacology at the City University of New York Medical School. Lynn Zimmer is a sociologist at Queens College at City University in New York. Morgan and Zimmer are coauthors of *Marijuana Myths, Marijuana Facts* and are board members of the National Organization for the Reform of Marijuana Laws, which works to legalize marijuana.

Marijuana Use Can Lead to Other Drugs

Joseph A. Califano

In 1997, the National Center on Addiction and Substance Abuse at Columbia University (CASA) for the first time established the statistical relationship between use of tobacco, alcohol, and marijuana—in and of themselves—and use of harder drugs such as cocaine, heroin and acid. (Virtually all teens who smoke marijuana also smoke nicotine cigarettes and drink alcohol.)

Compelling Correlations

Examining the data from the U.S. Centers for Disease Control and Prevention's 1995 Youth Risk Behavior Survey of 11,000 ninth- through 12th-graders, CASA isolated teen use of these gateway drugs from other problem behaviors, such as fighting, drunk driving, truancy, promiscuous sexual activity, carrying a weapon and attempting suicide. The correlations are compelling:

- Among teens who report no other problem behaviors, those who drank and smoked cigarettes at least once in the past month are 30 times likelier to smoke marijuana than those who didn't.
- Among teens with no other problem behaviors, those who used cigarettes, alcohol and marijuana at least once in the past month are almost 17 times likelier to use another drug like cocaine, heroin or acid.

Though only statistical, those relationships are powerful. For perspective, remember that in 1964 the first Surgeon General's Report on smoking and health found a nine to 10 times greater risk of lung cancer among smokers, and the early results of the Framingham heart study found that individuals with high cholesterol were two to four times likelier to suffer heart disease. Most who smoke marijuana do not move on to other drugs, just as most who smoke cigarettes do not get lung cancer; but both kinds of smokers enormously increase their risks. And those risks rise with teen use: the earlier and more often an individual uses marijuana, the likelier that person is to use cocaine.

Marijuana and Addiction

Recent biomedical research suggests the reasons why. Studies in Italy reveal that marijuana affects levels of dopamine (the substance that gives pleasure) in the brain in a manner similar to heroin. Gaetana DiChiara, who led this work at the University of Cagliari, indicates that marijuana may prime the brain to seek substances such as heroin and cocaine that act in a similar way. Studies in the United States have found that nicotine and cocaine also affect dopamine levels.

While psychological dependence on marijuana has been widely recognized, the drug's potential for physical addiction is only recently becoming clear. A team at Scripps Research Institute in California and Complutense University in Madrid found that rats subjected to immediate cannabis withdrawal exhibited changes in behavior similar to those seen after withdrawal of cocaine, alcohol and opiates. *Science* magazine called this, "the first neurological basis for marijuana withdrawal syndrome, and one with a strong emotional component that is shared by other drugs." Dr. Alan Leshner, the Director of the National Institute on Drug Abuse, estimates that more than 100,000 individuals

> The earlier and more often an individual uses marijuana, the likelier that person is to use cocaine.

are in treatment because of marijuana use. Most are believed to be teenagers.

We have known for some time that marijuana can damage ability to concentrate, short-term memory and motor skills when teens most need these attributes, when they are learning in school and developing rapidly. Now a body of work indicates marijuana as physically addictive and demonstrates that teens who play with the fire of cigarettes, alcohol and marijuana increase the danger that they will get burned by the flames of heroin, cocaine and acid. These findings make a strong case to start calling marijuana what it is: a hard drug, one that can bring serious harm to children and ruin their lives. . . .

The statistical link between smoking pot and using heroin, cocaine and acid, the indications that marijuana acts on dopamine levels in the brain in a manner similar to harder drugs and nicotine, and mounting evidence of marijuana's addictive power present a convincing case for a billion-dollar-a-year investment to move biomedical research on substance abuse and addiction into the big leagues at the National Institutes of Health, along with heart disease, cancer and AIDS.

Excerpted from "Marijuana: It's a Hard Drug," by Joseph A. Califano, editorial published in several newspapers September 30, 1997, and available at www.casacolumbia.org/newsletter1457/newsletter_show.htm?doc_id=6990. Reprinted by permission of the author and the Center on Addiction and Substance Abuse.

The Myth of Marijuana's Gateway Effect

John P. Morgan and Lynn Zimmer

The Partnership for a Drug-Free America, in cooperation with the National Institute on Drug Abuse (NIDA) and the White House Office of Drug Control Policy, recently announced a new anti-drug campaign that specifically targets marijuana. Instead of featuring horror tales of marijuana-induced insanity, violence and birth defects, this campaign is built upon the premise that reducing marijuana use is a practical strategy for reducing the use of more dangerous drugs.

Dan Wasserman © 1995 The Boston Globe. Reprinted by permission of Tribune Media Services.

The primary basis for this "gateway hypothesis" is a recent report by the Center on Addiction and Substance Abuse (CASA), claiming that marijuana users are 85 times more likely than non-marijuana users to try cocaine. This figure, using data from NIDA's 1991 National Household Survey on Drug Abuse, is close to being meaningless. It was calculated by dividing the proportion of marijuana users who have ever used cocaine (17%) by the proportion of cocaine users who have never used marijuana (.2%). The high risk-factor obtained is a product not of the fact that so many marijuana users use cocaine but that so many cocaine users used marijuana previously.

It is hardly a revelation that people who use one of the least popular drugs are likely to use the more popular ones—not only marijuana, but also alcohol and tobacco cigarettes. The obvious statistic not publicized by CASA is that most marijuana users—83 percent—never use cocaine. Indeed, for the nearly 70 million Americans who have tried marijuana, it is clearly a "terminus" rather than a "gateway" drug. . . .

Marijuana and Cocaine
Since the 1970s, when NIDA first began gathering data, rates of marijuana and cocaine use have displayed divergent patterns. Marijuana prevalence increased throughout the 1970s, peaking in 1979, when about 60 percent of high school seniors reported having used it at least once. During the 1980s, cocaine use increased while marijuana use was declining. Since 1991, when data for the CASA analysis were gathered, marijuana use-rates have increased while cocaine use-rates have remained fairly steady.

> For . . . 70 million Americans who have tried marijuana, it is clearly a "terminus" rather than a "gateway" drug.

The over-changing nature of the statistical relationship between use-rate for marijuana and cocaine indicates the absence of a causal link between the use of these two drugs. Therefore, even if the proposed Partnership campaign were to be effective in reducing marijuana use it would not guarantee a proportional reduction in the number of people who use cocaine. To the extent anti-drug cam-

paigns are effective, they seem to be most effective in de-
terring those people who would have been fairly low-level
users. There is no reason to believe that anti-marijuana
messages of any sort would deter many of those marijuana
users—currently 17 percent of the total—who also develop
an interest in cocaine.

Nor is there reason to believe that the Partnership's new
campaign will actually reduce the overall number of marijuana users. For a decade now, American youth have been
subjected to an unparalleled assault of anti-drug messages.
They have seen hundreds of Partnership advertisements,
on television and in the print media. They have been urged
to "just say no" by rock stars, sports heroes, presidents and
first ladies. They have been exposed to anti-drug educational programs in the schools. Yet this is the same generation of young people that recently began increasing its
use of marijuana. It seems unlikely that many of them will
be deterred by hyperbolic claims of marijuana's gateway
effect, particularly when it contradicts the reality of drug
use they see around them. . . .

A Rhetorical Tool

In the United States, the claim that marijuana acts as a
gateway to the use of other drugs serves mainly as a rhetor-
ical tool for frightening Americans into believing that win-
ning the war against heroin and cocaine requires waging a
battle against the casual use of marijuana. Not only is the
claim intellectually indefensible, but the battle is wasteful
of resources and fated to failure.

Excerpted from "The Myth of Marijuana's Gateway Effect," by John P. Morgan and Lynn Zimmer, *NORML's Active Resistance*, Spring 1995. Reprinted
by permission of the authors.

Chapter 3

Consequences of Using and Abusing Drugs

An Emergency Physician Describes Some Health Consequences of Drug Abuse

Nancy J. Auer

Many teens who abuse drugs sooner or later end up in a hospital emergency room, according to Nancy J. Auer, an emergency physician and vice president for medical affairs at Swedish Medical Center in Seattle, Washington. The following is taken from testimony she presented before Congress while serving as president of the American College of Emergency Physicians. She describes her experiences and those of fellow doctors in treating emergency patients whose lives had been threatened and in some cases ended by drugs.

As emergency physicians, we deal with a variety of drug- and alcohol-related cases on a daily basis. Although teenage drinking remains a very serious problem and is often used in combination with other drugs, there are other sinister and deadly drugs being used by the youth of America that I want to tell you about today.

Excerpted from Nancy J. Auer's testimony before the U.S. Senate Committee on the Judiciary, June 17, 1998.

Teenage drug use is indeed a growing crisis. According to the Drug Abuse Warning Network (DAWN), which tracks drug-related episodes in emergency departments—there were close to half a million drug-related episodes seen in emergency departments in 1996. Nearly 95,000 of these cases were young people between the ages of 18 and 25.

In 1995, a study published in *Annals of Emergency Medicine* found that patients who present to the emergency department with chest pain have often used cocaine. The study found that this was true for nearly one-third of the patients who were 18 to 30 years of age. This too demonstrates the prevalence of drug use among our youth. Ten years ago, I might not have asked an otherwise physically fit young person with chest pain if they were using drugs. Today it would be at the top of my list.

It takes time to publish an article and to track statistics. I want to share with you what is happening today in our communities. The illicit use of drugs is spreading downward from the high schools, to junior high—even to grade schools. And it's not just a problem of the poor, minorities, or inner-city residents. Drug users come into the emergency department from all walks of life and all parts of the country, including our more affluent, suburban neighborhoods. . . .

Personal Experiences

Let me share with you some of my own personal experiences and those of my fellow emergency physicians.

Recently, I treated a 19-year-old male who came to the emergency department experiencing severe chest pain and shortness of breath. This young man was having a heart attack as a result of cocaine use. In a 55-year-old male, a heart attack is typically the result of clogged arteries. In the case of a young cocaine user, the arteries go into spasms depriving the heart of oxygen. The result is cardiac arrest, permanent heart damage and possibly death. Although this young man lived, his life has been changed forever. He's a cardiac cripple. His activities are severely restricted and he's at risk of premature death.

I had another teen—a child really. Fourteen years old, brought in by medics because he had flipped his skateboard over a concrete bridge and dropped 12 feet to the pavement below. You see, he was high on speed and thought he could fly. Fortunately, he was not badly hurt, but while in the treatment room, he became very agitated and thought the restraints placed on him to protect his neck and back meant we were trying to put him in jail. He tore off the restraints and struck a nurse in an effort to escape.

> There were close to half a million drug-related episodes seen in emergency departments in 1996.

In another recent case, I treated a 17-year-old heroin user. She had made repeated visits to the emergency department for drug use. She had started taking recreational drugs at age 14. On her last visit, she was 7 months pregnant and overdosed on heroin, barely breathing. After we rescued her, I talked her into quitting for her and her baby's sake. Fortunately, I was able to get her into Washington State's Medicaid drug treatment program for pregnant women where she and her baby could receive appropriate drug treatment and medical care. The baby, however, may be born with brain damage from the mother's drug abuse.

Stories from Other Emergency Physicians

In Billings, Montana, in a case reported by my colleague Dr. Larry McEvoy in *Time* magazine, a boy [on methamphetamine or "crank"] was treated in the emergency department who was so out of control he thought emergency department staff were police trying to kill or kidnap him. The boy was incredibly violent—biting, slapping, and grabbing doctors' private parts. Emergency department staff contacted the teen's parents who told him the boy was basically a good kid and a good student. However, as Dr. McEvoy said, even if the teenager does this once every 2 years, given his psychotic reaction to the drug, he could end up killing someone.

In Plano, an affluent suburb of Dallas, Texas, over the last 19 months [prior to June 1998], there have been 100 teenage heroin overdoses, resulting in 25 deaths. The heroin that caused these deaths is a powdered form, known as "chiva," or "black tar," which can be smoked or snorted. One of the most tragic cases related to me by Dr. Larry Alexander involved a 16-year-old boy who was at a party snorting this dangerous drug. Without his friends noticing, he slumped in a corner. An hour later, they discovered he had vomited and stopped breathing. They dragged him down three flights of stairs, threw him in a car and drove to the nearest emergency department, where they dumped him and went back to the party. After trying to resuscitate him, the boy died and Dr. Alexander had to call the boy's parents in the middle of the night with the phone call that every parent hopes they never get—the call from the emergency department that your child has died.

> Young people . . . have . . . had their lives drastically altered or ended by drugs.

We know why this child died. He died from a heroin overdose. But what's it really like to die from heroin? Let me tell you, it's not a pretty scene. First, you experience a euphoric high, overall body warmth and mellow out. Your senses become heightened, but then the lights start becoming too bright. Sounds become too loud and smells too strong. Your body becomes heavy and your tongue becomes thick. You feel nauseated and vomit. Because the heroin paralyzes your gag reflexes, the vomit goes into your windpipe and into your lungs, and you suffocate. Then your heart stops.

In Mt. Pleasant, Texas, with a population of approximately 10,000, Dr. Brad Burrows tells me they have been seeing six to eight medical emergencies a month related to cocaine use and two to three emergencies a month related to methamphetamine use. This hospital draws from a very rural area in east Texas. . . .

Dr. Susan Nedza, an emergency physician practicing in an affluent Chicago suburb, has seen an increase in heroin overdoses and addiction among young adults and teens, ranging from 16 to 24 years of age. Many of these patients are under the false impression that if they don't inject heroin and only snort it, they will not be harmed or become addicted. They are wrong. They are white, well educated, from good homes and still have become addicted.

A National Crisis

These are only a few of the cases emergency physicians see every day, but the effects of illegal drug use extend far beyond the walls of the emergency department and into family life, schoolrooms, and violence on our streets. Addressing the problem of teenage drug use will take a national, as well as community-wide effort, involving not only the medical community and law enforcement, but parents, teachers, ministers, and other community leaders. . . .

We must face the problem of teenage drug use head on, at all levels—in government and in the private sector. One of the most painful experiences I can have as an emergency physician is telling parents their child has died from a drug overdose. And this is happening far too often in America today.

The young people I've told you about today have all had their lives drastically altered or ended by drugs. This could just have easily been your child, niece, nephew or grandchild. But, any child is really OUR child and OUR future. We must all work together to end this growing crisis in America.

The Connection Between Drugs and AIDS

National Institute on Drug Abuse

The following piece by the National Institute on Drug Abuse (NIDA) focuses on one particular risk of drug use—the possibility of contracting AIDS, a sexually transmitted disease that is often fatal. Taking drugs can cloud a person's judgment or make it harder for a person to resist unwanted sexual advances. This in turn can make someone more likely to engage in risky or unprotected sex, thus risking AIDS.

B eing a teen is exciting. Being a teen in a world with drugs, sex, and AIDS, is hard.

You might not know all the ways drugs and AIDS are connected.

This article will help you understand the dangers and how to avoid them. Drugs, like alcohol, marijuana, and cocaine can cloud your judgment, make it hard to know right from wrong, distract you from reality.

Drugs Make You Forget What's Important . . . so you care less about yourself or your friends, because, you just don't care.

You Forget You're Only Human. When you get high you may mistakenly believe nothing bad could happen to you.

Drugs Can Make You Do Things You May Wish You Never Did, Like:

Reprinted from *Get High, Get Stupid, Get AIDS*, by the National Institute on Drug Abuse, NIH Publication No. 94-3881, available online at www.health.org/govpubs/PHD573/index.htm.

- act reckless and foolish
- get romantic with someone you don't really like
- have sex without planning
- have sex without thinking of the consequences
- forget to use a condom or forget to have your partner use a condom.

When Drugs Make You Forget, You May Take Risks, Like Having Sex. Teen years are a time of making all kinds of new decisions. One of those decisions is when to have sex. It's important to make that decision with a clear head because sex today is far riskier than ever before. Drugs, like alcohol, marijuana, and cocaine can get in the way of making clear decisions.

Why Is Sex Risky? It Can Lead to AIDS.
- Unprotected sex with an infected partner is the most common way HIV, the virus that causes AIDS, is spread. Another way is sharing needles to inject drugs.
- Your sex partner may have had sex with someone who shared a needle to inject drugs with an HIV infected person.
- The more sex partners you have, the more chance you have of getting AIDS.
- Two sure ways to avoid the AIDS virus are: not having sex and not sharing needles.
- If you choose to have sex, always use a condom to help reduce the risk of getting AIDS.

Make Your Decision About Sex With a Clear Head, Without Drugs. Sometimes you can feel pressured to have sex when you may not want to, and drugs make it harder to say no. Pressure about sex can be hard to deal with—it can come from your boyfriend or girlfriend, from the crowd you hang out with, or even from your own feelings.

The first thing to remember is you're in charge of your body and what you choose to do with it.

The second thing to remember is there is a lot at stake—a decision about sex can have consequences that last a lifetime.

It Helps to Make a Plan and Stick to it. Then if someone offers you drugs or suggested sex, you'll know what to do. Plan not to use drugs so you can keep a clear head. Plan how to say no, to be careful, and to think about what to do. The time to make your plan is when you have a clear head.

Making Your Plan. Think about who you are and what's important to you, think about how using drugs and having sex could affect that. When you have a plan it's easier to handle situations where you want to have fun with friends but don't want to use drugs or have sex.

> Sometimes you can feel pressured to have sex when you may not want to, and drugs make it harder to say no.

If someone pressures you about drugs you can say nicely but firmly, "I'm not interested," or, "I don't use drugs."

If someone pressures you about sex you could let them know where you stand by saying: "I'm not ready for it yet," or, "Maybe it feels right for you, but it's not for me."

It's a Fact.

- Teens who use condoms during sex tend to use them less if they've been drinking or smoking dope.
- More than 20 percent of the people who have AIDS are in their 20's. Since it can take up to 10 years or more for symptoms to start, many got infected in their teens.
- The number of reported AIDS cases among teenagers increased 96% between 1988 and 1990.

You May Already Know This But . . .

- YOU CANNOT GET AIDS from hugging, holding hands, mosquitoes or bugs.
- YOU CAN GET AIDS from unprotected sexual contact.
- HIV is the human immunodeficiency virus that causes AIDS.
- You cannot tell someone has the HIV virus by looking at them. A blood test is the only way to be sure.
- AIDS is fatal.

Legal Consequences of Illegal Drug Use

Cynthia Kuhn, Scott Swartzwelder, and Wilkie Wilson

Most recreational drugs are illegal to possess, sell, or consume. The United States has passed strict laws and has waged an aggressive police campaign against drug trafficking. Because of the "war on drugs," the legal consequences of getting caught with illegal drugs can be devastating, write the authors of *Buzzed,* a reference work on drugs that is excerpted here. Cynthia Kuhn and Wilkie Wilson are professors of pharmacology at Duke University Medical Center. Scott Swartzwelder is a psychology professor at Duke University.

It is said that your life can change forever in a matter of seconds. When a person mixes drugs and the legal system, the combination can easily become life-changing. For a variety of reasons, the lawmaking bodies of most countries, especially the United States, have decided to suppress drug use by making drug laws harsh and certain. All who deal with drugs in an illegal manner are thus at risk for penalties that can disrupt their own lives and those of their families. . . .

Many . . . drugs are illegal in all circumstances—manufactur-

Excerpted from *Buzzed: The Straight Facts About the Most Used and Abused Drugs from Alcohol to Ecstasy,* by Cynthia Kuhn, Scott Swartzwelder, and Wilkie Wilson. Copyright © 1998 by Cynthia Kuhn, Scott Swartzwelder, and Wilkie Wilson. Used by permission of W.W. Norton & Company, Inc.

ing, distribution, and possession. Others are legal when pre-scribed, but not for recreational use. Still others, such as alcohol, can be legal, but their use is prohibited for activities such as driving a car or operating a boat.

[The following] is written to inform readers about very basic laws and principles that come into play around drug issues. It is not intended to give advice about dealing with the law-enforcement community or the judicial system. If you feel that you need that advice, find a good lawyer and ask her all of your questions before you become legally involved.

The Principles

1. Everyone wants to know about the laws regarding the rights of a law officer to search one's car or one's home. This is a very complicated issue that is often decided in the courts in individual cases. Generally one has the greatest "expecta-tion of privacy" in one's home. There is less expectation of privacy in a car, and the least when one is out in public.

2. If a law-enforcement officer suspects you of a crime and really wants to search you or your car, you will be searched, whether or not you give permission. If you give your permission, the search will almost certainly be con-sidered legal. If you refuse permission, the search may or may not be legal, but it may happen anyway. The debate over whether the search was permitted and legal will begin in the court system. The easiest way to avoid trouble is to avoid situations in which a random and unexpected search will yield anything illegal.

3. A person who is innocent of any crime, but is with some-one arrested for possessing drugs, may become involved with the legal system until her innocence is proven. By that time, she may have hired an expensive lawyer, terrified her family, and spent some time under arrest.

4. The penalties for drug-related activities can be horrendous,

especially in the United States federal judicial system, and particularly for selling drugs. Many casual drug users do not realize that simple possession of a modest amount of a drug can automatically be considered "intent to distribute," whether or not one actually plans to sell the drug.

5. One does not have to be on government property to be in violation of federal law. The federal drug laws apply every-where in the United States at all times.

6. State and federal laws can be extremely strict about the use of guns in the commission of crimes. The possession of a gun—even having one just in the vicinity of a crime—can add many years onto the sentence for the original crime.

7. Many people believe that they are "safe" from serious le-gal consequences because they know the local officials, or because they believe the penalties are not serious. They are wrong. First, an arrest by a state or local officer can easily be referred to federal prosecutors not subject to local po-litical influence. Second, in many states and in the federal system there is no parole. Even worse, "guideline" or "structured" sentencing laws give the judges practically no leeway for reduced sentences.

8. Finally, remember that while one may have and know one's rights as a citizen, those rights do not apply in for-eign countries, and the legal consequences of drug-law violations in some places can literally mean death. . . .

Illegal Acts

The drug laws are complicated, and the states differ from each other and from the federal system. So, there is no easy way to explain them in detail. However, there are a few very powerful and relatively unknown aspects of the law that should be ex-plained to everyone.

First is the difference between a felony and a misdemeanor. A misdemeanor is a minor crime that might result in a fine, a public service, or a short prison sentence. A felony is considered such a serious crime that convicted individuals lose many rights that ordinary citizens enjoy. This includes the right to hold many kinds of highly paid jobs. A felony conviction is truly a life-changing event. Understanding this is important for drug users because possession of some amounts of some drugs can be considered a misdemeanor, while larger amounts are always felonies.

> All who deal with drugs in an illegal manner are . . . at risk for penalties that can disrupt their own lives.

The law always sets the level of punishment based on the amount of a drug that one possesses or distributes, and in this case size counts a lot. For example, there is a current public controversy because the federal laws are terribly tough for possession of even a few grams of crack cocaine, but one would have to possess much more powdered cocaine to receive the same punishment. Anyone who contemplates drug usage should understand the severity of the penalties that various levels of drug possession invoke.

Most people know that conviction for selling drugs (distribution) results in stiffer penalties than for possession. What they don't know is that simply possessing certain amounts of a drug can be considered "intent to distribute," and thus may subject the person to the much stiffer distribution penalties. Moreover, money may not have to change hands for distribution to take place from a legal perspective. Simply handing a package of a drug from one person to another can be considered distribution. . . .

We cannot stress enough the seriousness with which the law-making bodies are taking drug issues. The drug penalties get more severe every day. . . .

Getting Caught

Most people believe that it will not happen to them. Teenagers, in particular, have the feeling that they are "beyond the law." But it does happen. It happens to grandmothers, teenagers, lawyers, doctors, and the most ordinary people on the face of the earth. . . .

The law-enforcement community is actually quite sophisticated in its drug-enforcement efforts. Drug Enforcement Administration agents work all over the world trying to prevent the transport of drugs into the United States. They have agents working major and minor airports, and even the bus stations. The highway patrols of most states have drug interdiction units looking for suspicious vehicles. This is not a trivial effort, and it results in so many convictions that both the state and federal prison populations have grown dramatically in the last fifteen years.

> Many people believe . . . they are "safe" from serious legal consequences. . . . They are wrong.

Yet everyone realizes that most countries are overrun with drugs. It is usually easy to buy the most common illegal drugs in many areas of cities and on college campuses. So why is the legal interdiction effort perceived as failing? It is not exactly failing, but rather it is being overwhelmed. Many, many people are caught in the legal system, but there is always someone else to replace each person caught. Routine usage of cocaine, crack, or heroin can be a very expensive habit, and the only way that most people can maintain such expensive behavior is to turn to dealing. . . . The combination of dependence and expense often leads users to become dealers until they are stopped by medical intervention, arrest, or death.

What does this have to do with . . . [you]? . . . [You] no doubt [have] the ability to do honest and legal work and have a successful life. . . . [You] might feel that [you are] above being caught, or just not in the right "circle of friends" to be caught. This might be the most dangerous attitude of all, because, like most jobs, illegal drug dealing depends on knowledge, skills, and having a network of people. Most casual dealers do not have the knowledge or, fortunately, are not willing to do what is necessary to involve themselves fully in the drug culture. Thus, they approach the whole issue as amateurs, and, like many amateurs in anything, they fail miserably. Only in this case, the stakes are much higher. They can get caught, lose a lot of money, become victims of criminal violence, or become heavily dependent on the substance they are dealing.

As we all know, some people think they have few opportunities and only a short time to live. They will deal drugs no matter what anyone says. In their lives they see jail time as just the cost of doing business. However, a district attorney who has prosecuted thousands of drug cases had just one bit of advice: people with families, an opportunity for education, and a supportive network of friends have so much to lose from being on the wrong side of the legal system that they should never become involved with it. A felony conviction can strip a person of so many opportunities in this society, and can cost families so much in pain, suffering, and financial loss, that no amount of money or drug experience is worth the risk.

How Drugs Can Lead to Trouble—A Teen's Story

Richard Robart, as told to Janice Arenofsky

A fifteen-year-old tells his story of how drugs have affected his life. After becoming involved with drugs at the age of 11, he began to skip school, steal, and get into fights. Eventually he developed a criminal record and was forced to confront his drug addiction.

I started on drugs the summer after sixth grade, when I was just 11. One of my friends bought some marijuana, and four of us kids smoked it at his house. Everyone was doing it, so I did too.

The first time, I didn't feel anything, but the second time I did. Smoking marijuana didn't make me think about anything unpleasant. I'd just laugh. I'd also use alcohol—the hard stuff. Sometimes I'd do both at the same time, but I was smoking more than drinking.

In the beginning, I smoked pot once every two weeks. But eventually I did it almost every day. At first I didn't feel addicted. It was just something I wanted to do. But then I started getting dependent—the need for it got into my head and stayed there.

Reprinted, with permission, from "Drugs Can Turn Cool Kids into Criminals," by Janice Arenofsky, *Current Health 1®*, December 1999. Copyright © 1999 and published by Weekly Reader Corporation. All rights reserved.

Addiction Led to Crime

I'd smoke in the street with my friends, or we'd go to a friend's house. I'd come home high with red eyes and I'd feel real tired. I also couldn't talk well because my mouth felt dry and cottony. My dad suspected drugs.

I didn't really go to school when I was taking drugs. I'd ditch classes, or I wouldn't pay attention. I was kicked out of two high schools for fighting. I also stole things like candy and cigarettes from cars and stores. I sold them at school for drug money.

Eventually I got arrested. I was locked up at the Durango Juvenile Facility in Phoenix for a month. It was real hard for me in jail. There were gangs and a lot of fights. Even though you went to school in the morning, you'd have to stay on your unit for the rest of the day, and there was nothing to do.

Running Away from Help

Then I was sent to New Foundation, a rehabilitation clinic in Scottsdale, Arizona. But I still wasn't ready to get off drugs. I ran away from this facility for a week with a couple of friends.

When I was on the run, I got high and drank. We did some stupid things. Once at a convenience store, we were so drunk on beer, we backed up and hit another car. We took off from the parking lot with the car chasing us. We flew 50 mph through this intersection and sped down the streets. We could have died.

During that week I also saw how tough it was to get money. I thought it would be easy, but it wasn't. It also wasn't fun. Finally I decided I didn't want to live like that. So I turned myself back in to New Foundation.

Figuring Things Out

I attended school there every day until 2:30 in the afternoon. Then we met in small groups. Going to group meetings helped. I found out some of the reasons I started doing drugs. I had a lot of anger that I wasn't dealing with. I was angry because my mom kidnapped me from my dad when I was little. And I was angry at my dad because he did a lot of drugs himself when I was growing up. So I pretty much had to take care of myself. I shared a lot of my feelings with other kids there and also talked with my dad.

I'm off drugs now, but I have a juvenile record. I'm also on probation for the next 10 months. I've got a job installing satellite dishes and solar heating units, and I have a new girlfriend who doesn't use drugs. (My ex-girlfriend started doing drugs, so I broke up with her.) And I'm returning to a regular high school. The principal said he'll let me back: But if I mess up, then I'm out for good.

> I didn't really go to school when I was taking drugs.

It was easy to get into drugs. They're all over. If you're just walking down the street, someone can come up to you and ask you if you want to buy a "sack." Little kids sell marijuana in school or in the park. You can be out riding your bike around the streets and someone can approach you.

I try now to avoid being with people who use drugs. But sometimes I'm around it, and you just have to say no. I had the chance to get into harder drugs, but when I see people tripping off of them, I don't see any fun in it. And they are sick the next day too.

Words of Advice

If I had everything to do over again, I'd stick to sports, such as bike racing. I'd also choose better friends. You need to keep busy and not get bored. That's what I tell my kid sister. Find something you like to do and do it. Don't just hang out, because then you're looking for trouble.

These days I play basketball after work and go to Narcotics Anonymous meetings. I'm planning to graduate high school, get a basketball or football scholarship, and go to college. Now that I'm out of drugs, I'm into sports, and I'm pretty good at them.

Drugs and Family Life

Osei K. Edwards

One thing teens should keep in mind when deciding whether to use marijuana or other drugs is the effect their decision may have on their family life, writes high school student Osei K. Edwards. Parents and other relatives may react in different ways to the discovery that their children smoke pot, he writes, but few are happy about it. In some cases family relationships may be destroyed. Edwards writes for *New Youth Connections*, a New York-based youth publication.

I magine it's late at night and you're snoozing in bed when all of a sudden, your mother storms into your room like she's on a mission. She pulls you out of bed, yanks your ears and starts screaming.

"Oh Lord, get the devil out of my child. Forgive him for he knows not what he's doing."

Why would your mother turn into a psalm-spouting fanatic (she's not even religious), ruin your slumber (and your ears), and make you feel like you just killed the Easter Bunny? Because she found weed in your coat pocket and she thinks you're possessed by demons, that's why.

Parents react in a lot of different ways when they realize their

Reprinted from "Family Feuds," by Osei K. Edwards, *New Youth Connections*, May/June 1996, by permission of *New Youth Connections*. Copyright © 1996 by Youth Communication, 224 W. 29th St., 2nd Fl., New York, NY 10001.

kids smoke marijuana. The teens I spoke to told me stories about everything from getting kicked out of the house to having parents who gave them their very first taste of weed at an early age.

Carl, 17, . . . said his room "smells like air freshener, cheap cologne, incense and chronic." He says he thinks that's why his mother suspects something's up. "[She] asked me if I want help or rehab," he said.

Carl's father, on the other hand, chooses to look the other way. "Since my father's job involves law," he explained, "[as long as] he doesn't see it . . . [there's] no evidence."

> The majority of people I interviewed said that their families aren't all that happy about their smoking.

But other people's parents are much stricter and less trusting once they find out their child smokes weed. "My mother kicked me out [for a while]," said Albert, 18, . . . "She doesn't like giving me money like she used to." John, 17, . . . said his mother "be thinking I'm high and drunk all the time when I come home late."

And while these parents may have laid down the law when it comes to smoking weed, not all parents seem to mind. Mona, 17, . . . says if her parents found out, "they wouldn't care . . . they both smoke it."

Some people grow up around family members who smoke—parents, uncles, brothers, cousins. "Kenaz," 17, . . . is a chip off the ol' block. "My father offered it to me while he was bunin' with his brethren," he said. "I was 5 years old."

Albert was in junior high when one day he was "chillin'" in a car with his favorite uncle who was "passing around a spliff" with his friends. Albert was only supposed to pass it to the next person but instead he "took about four pulls."

Later on, he went to the same uncle's house and, instead of giving Albert a hard time, his uncle used a different tactic to try to discourage him from smoking.

Reverse Psychology

"[My uncle] said he's gonna make me quit by giving me so much that it will backfire," said Albert. "We had four ells and a 22 of Heineken . . . I was redd out of my mind . . . I couldn't walk home. I had to take a cab." Nevertheless, his uncle was unsuccessful in turning Albert off weed.

There were a few exceptions but the majority of the people I interviewed said that their families aren't all that happy about their smoking. "My family doesn't condone it," said Albert. "But it's my life, and there is nothin' they can do about it."

I agree, it is his life, but I also believe that family can be a very important part of your life. Risking those unique and once-in-a-lifetime relationships over something that just makes you feel cool for a brief period of time is something worth thinking about. The choice is yours.

Marijuana and Driving

Judy Monroe

A potentially fatal consequence of drug abuse is the increased likelihood of automobile accidents. Judy Monroe, a journalist, reports on the effects of marijuana on driving ability. She writes that marijuana can impair a person's judgment, concentration, and reaction time, especially when taken in combination with alcohol. Monroe also records one teenager's experiences with marijuana and driving.

"At age 18, I was living with my sister and her family. I didn't have much privacy there, so my friends and I got high on pot [marijuana] in our cars a lot." Sunnie R. paused.

"I remember the first time I got high. It was the night of the January earthquake. My girlfriend was driving along the 405 freeway in California, and I was in the backseat. My friends were passing around a bong—it's like a waterpipe that concentrates a lot of marijuana smoke. The first time I tried it, the smoke made me cough and burned my throat and lungs. After another hit, I didn't care about the pain, as I got high."

Sunnie began to smoke pot regularly, with friends or by herself. "As a result of using pot, I got absentminded. I constantly forgot to turn off my car lights and would wear down the battery. Or I'd forget to change the oil and almost burned out the engine several times. Expensive car repairs piled up.

Reprinted, with permission, from "How Marijuana Affects Driving," by Judy Monroe, *Current Health 2*®, May 1997. Copyright © 1997 and published by Weekly Reader Corporation. All rights reserved.

"One time when I was high, I really messed up my sister's car. Pot slows down your motor reflexes, so it's hard to operate a car. I kept trying to park her car and got too close to a wall and ruined the outside with scratches and dings all over. She was so mad at me.

"Pot also impairs your ability to make good judgment calls. The drug convinces you that you're making good choices. Instead, I'd do such stupid things. I'd drive around by myself in very unsafe areas and do dumb things like forgetting where I was. I'd mistake people for shadows and nearly hit them.

"One night, my car transmission went out in a bad area. I sat there for two hours, scared to flag down the police because if they realized I was high, I could go to jail. I finally fell asleep, and when I woke up the next morning, someone had stolen my hubcaps, but I was OK. My brother-in-law was furious when he came and got me."

> Studies have shown that marijuana plays a role in crashes.

Her family called a meeting the next day and told Sunnie she had to get help. "By this time, I was in bad shape. Marijuana had taken away my goals, dreams, and desires. I was living minute-to-minute," Sunnie says.

Drugs and Driving Don't Mix

Studies have shown that marijuana plays a role in crashes. And when users combine marijuana with alcohol, the hazards of driving can be more severe than with either drug alone.

Marijuana affects drivers' ability to focus, visually follow, and pay attention to what is going on around their vehicle. Drivers who are high become disoriented. This increases the chances of missing turning cars or cars entering a highway from a ramp. Marijuana decreases peripheral vision and can affect depth perception, so drivers may miss seeing cars or pedestrians off to the side. Because distances seem longer and objects may seem larger, drivers who are high may run into vehicles stopped at lights.

According to the National Institute on Drug Abuse, one study of patients in a hospital's shock-trauma unit who had been in traffic accidents found that 15 percent had been smoking marijuana; 17 percent had both alcohol and THC (delta-9-

How Other Drugs Affect Driving

Drug Type	How They Affect Driving
Prescription	
Antidepressants, including Prozac, Paxil, Zoloft, Serzone, Effoxor, amitriptyline	Can make users drowsy, less alert
Codeine-based pain relievers for sore throat, dental work	Make users drowsy, less alert; slow reflexes
Prescription or over-the-counter	
Antihistamines for allergies and breathing problems	Can make users drowsy, less alert
Illegal	
Narcotics, including heroin and morphine	Drowsiness, lethargy
Hallucinogens, including LSD and mescaline	Altered sense of time, space, and reality; decreased concentration, reaction time, and coordination; confusion; disorientation
Stimulants, including cocaine, crack, methamphetamine, amphetamines	Violent, erratic, or paranoid behavior; disorientation
Depressants, including alcohol (illegal under age 21) and barbiturates	Dulling of senses; double vision; dizziness; impaired coordination, reflexes, judgment, and decision making
Inhalants	Forgetfulness, delayed reflexes, dizziness

Current Health 2, May 1997.

tetrahydrocannabinol, the main active chemical in marijuana) in their blood.

Effects on the Body

Marijuana affects people differently. Some may feel nothing when they first try it. Others may feel high or intoxicated, as if they're drunk. Because they're so relaxed and drowsy, they may fall asleep behind the wheel.

Users often become engrossed with ordinary sights, sounds, or tastes, and minor events may seem extremely interesting or funny. This is bad news for drivers. Users don't focus on driving and instead may get wrapped up in music on the radio, for example.

> When high, the person is more likely to make mistakes.

While high, time seems to pass slowly, so minutes seem like hours. Users tend to have poor reaction times while driving, misjudging how long it takes to slow down or to stop the car.

Bad reactions can occur, especially with high doses of THC or if marijuana is mixed with other drugs such as cocaine. As Sunnie learned, "You never know what you're getting when you buy pot. Sometimes it's laced with cocaine, LSD, or speed."

Marijuana reacts quickly in the body. Within a few minutes, users develop dry mouth, rapid heartbeat, some loss of coordination, a poor sense of balance, and decreased reaction time. Blood vessels in the eye expand, making eyes look red. For some people, marijuana raises blood pressure.

THC can last a long time in the body because body fat absorbs THC. This means that urine testing can detect THC several days after a smoking session. In heavy, chronic users, the chemical can be detected for weeks or months, even if a person has stopped using marijuana.

When Sunnie used marijuana, she had trouble with thinking and problem-solving. These effects are typical of marijuana users.

Marijuana affects short-term memory—that is, memory of recent events. THC disrupts the nerve cells in the part of the brain where memories are formed. In turn, this makes it hard to learn while high.

When high, the person is more likely to make mistakes. The mistakes could be embarrassing or even cause a car crash. And like Sunnie, when people use marijuana a lot, they may lose energy and interest in school, work, family, and life.

Getting a Fresh Start

Once her family forced Sunnie to admit she was addicted to marijuana, she got help. With a lot of work, Sunnie stopped using marijuana. "I've been sober since April 1994." Now 21, Sunnie is rebuilding her life.

Marijuana and Your Grades

ForReal.org

What effect does smoking pot have on a person's school grades? Common sense should indicate that marijuana affects your brain and can get in the way of good grades, according to the following article from ForReal.org, a website on marijuana produced for teens by the Substance Abuse and Mental Health Services Administration. SAMHSA is an agency of the U.S. Department of Health and Human Services.

C *an using marijuana affect your grades?*
What's your best guess? Even someone who may not know or agree with the research on this topic could use a little common sense to answer this question. Not sure? Well, consider these facts:

Getting weed and then getting high takes time.

If someone is spending their time looking for and then smoking marijuana, they are obviously NOT studying. Between after-school jobs, sports, extra-curricular activities, family obligations, and some quality down time, it's already hard enough to find time to study. If someone is using that precious time to get high, chances are they won't do as well in school as someone who studies.

Reprinted from "Can Marijuana Affect Your Grades?" an online article on the ForReal.org website at www.forreal.org/think/affectgrade.asp.

The Connection Between Not Using Drugs and Receiving Good Grades

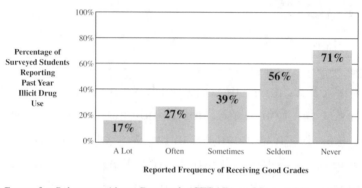

Center for Substance Abuse Research (CESAR) and Parents' Resource Institute for Drug Education (PRIDE), 1998.

Getting high is not the best way to get ready for a test.

No matter what the scientific studies say, some people still don't believe using marijuana impacts their memory. So let's forget the scientific stuff for a minute. Ask yourself this question: If your parents or another adult said they would buy you the car of your dreams if you aced your next biology exam, would you get high and then study for the test or opt to study drug free?

Marijuana and the Brain

Marijuana affects your brain.

Here are the uncontested scientific facts about how marijuana affects the brain you're counting on to get you that diploma. THC, the main active ingredient in marijuana, binds to and activates specific receptors, known as cannabinoid receptors. There are many of these receptors in parts of the brain that control memory, thought, concentration, time and depth perception, and coordinated movement. By activating these receptors, THC interferes with the normal functioning of the cerebellum, the part of the brain most responsible for balance, posture, and coordination of movement. The hippocampus, which is involved with memory formation, also contains many cannabinoid receptors. Studies have suggested that marijuana activates cannabinoid receptors in the hippocampus and affects memory by decreasing the activity of neurons in this area. The effect of marijuana on long-term memory is less certain, but while someone is under the influence of marijuana, short-term memory can be compromised. Further, research studies have shown chronic administration of THC can permanently damage the hippocampus of rats, suggesting that marijuana use can lead to permanent memory impairment. So, if you think a good memory can help you get good grades, using marijuana could definitely get in the way.

College-age marijuana users get lower grades than nonusers.

No one is saying that people who smoke marijuana are total losers. In fact, they were smart enough to get into college so this study could be done! But the study found that the college students who used marijuana got lower grades than students who didn't. . . .

The Bottom Line

The bottom line is that using marijuana can only make it harder for you to do your best—no matter how smart you are. You might know someone who smokes marijuana and still gets decent grades. But that person will never know how much farther they could have gone if they weren't smoking marijuana.

Point of Contention: Should Abstinence Be the Sole Goal of Drug Education Programs?

In the 1980s, first lady Nancy Reagan popularized the theme of "just say no" as the message society should tell teens about drugs. Since then, drug education programs, most of which receive some form of federal funding, have emphasized a "zero tolerance" outlook toward drug use. Students are told that any use of illegal drugs is unacceptable, are given information on the risks of drugs, and taught interpersonal skills to avoid them. While many parents and educators continue to support this approach, some question whether students should be taught more than "just say no." Critics of drug education programs argue that not all drug use constitutes abuse and that total abstinence may be an unrealistic goal for all teenagers. Some advocate a "harm reduction" approach to drug education that would provide teens information on how to minimize the risks and harms of drug use.

The following two selections present differing views on what students should be taught about drugs. The Lindesmith Center-Drug Policy Foundation is an organization that seeks to broaden the debate over drug policy in the United States. Sue Rusche is executive director of National Families in Action, a national drug education and policy center. Betty Sembler, a participant in the 1987 White House Conference for a Drug-Free America, founded the

Drug Free America Foundation, a nonprofit organization that works to educate Americans about drugs and controlled substance laws.

Abstinence Should Not Be the Sole Goal of Drug Education

The Lindesmith Center–Drug Policy Foundation

Since the 1960s, school-based drug prevention programs for adolescents have relied on scare tactics, zero tolerance, and "just say no." In 1998 the federal government spent $2.4 billion on prevention, and a new billion-dollar campaign has recently been launched. Still, by the time they graduate from high school, half of American teenagers will have used illegal drugs. Students often fail to take drug education programs seriously, doubting the validity of their information.

Many educators, health professionals, and parents are seeking alternatives that strongly promote abstinence while providing a fallback strategy of honest, science-based education for teenagers who say "maybe" or "sometimes" or "yes." This "Just Say Know" approach provides sound information as the basis for responsible decision-making, a reduction in drug abuse, and ultimately the promotion of safety.

Drug education has existed in America for over a century. It has utilized a variety of methods, from scare tactics to resistance techniques, in the effort to prevent young people from using drugs. Nonetheless, teenagers continue to experiment with a variety of substances. Despite the recent expansion of drug prevention programs, it is very difficult to know which, if any, "work" better than others. The assumptions that shape conventional programs render them problematic: that drug experimentation constitutes deviance; that drug use is the same as drug abuse; that marijuana constitutes the "gateway" to "harder" substances; that exaggeration of risks will deter experimentation.

The main reasons many students fail to take programs seriously, and continue to experiment with drugs, is that they have learned for themselves that America is hardly "drug-free"; there are vast differences between experimentation, abuse, and addiction; and the use of one drug does not inevitably lead to the use of others.

A Fallback Strategy

While youth abstinence is what we'd all prefer, this unrealistic goal means programs lack risk reduction education for those 50% who do not "just say no." We need a fallback strategy of safety first in order to prevent drug abuse and drug problems among teenagers.

Educational efforts should define "drugs" broadly, to include both illegal and legal substances. Programs should acknowledge teens' ability to make reasoned decisions; differentiate between use and abuse; and stress the importance of moderation and context. Curricula should be age-specific, stress student participation and provide science-based, objective educational materials. In simple terms, it is our responsibility as parents and teachers to engage students and provide them with credible information so they can make responsible decisions, avoid drug abuse, and stay safe.

> While youth abstinence is what we'd all prefer, this unrealistic goal means programs lack risk reduction education.

Reprinted, with permission, from "Drug Education," an article in the online library section of the Lindesmith Center–Drug Policy Foundation website at www.lindesmith.org/library/focal20.html.

Abstinence Should Be the Fundamental Goal of Drug Education

Sue Rusche and Betty Sembler

As if parents didn't have enough to worry about. Now comes something called "reality-based" drug education, and it's being pushed by the people who want us to legalize drugs.

These programs call for educators to teach children that they can have "healthy relationships" with marijuana, PCP, cocaine, crack and heroin, and that they can use these drugs "safely."

This approach to drug education is one thing that drove adolescent drug use up in the 1970s to the highest levels in history, from less than 1 percent in 1962 to 34 percent of adolescents, 65 percent of high school seniors and 70 percent of young adults by 1979.

High levels of drug use among teens also produced high levels of drug abuse, drug addiction and drug-related deaths. By 1979, 1 in 9 high school seniors smoked marijuana daily. Many needed drug treatment to stop. And so many teens died from drug and alcohol-related causes, their age group's life span actually decreased, while that of all other age groups lengthened.

In response, outraged parents organized some 4,000 drug-prevention groups nationwide. One of their first battles was to get rid of "responsible use" messages and replace them with clear, consistent no-use messages in drug-education programs, particularly those paid for with tax dollars.

The result? Between 1979 and 1992, regular drug use went down by half among all ages (from 25 million Americans to 12 million) and by two-thirds among adolescents and young adults.

Proponents of Drug Legalization

Now legalization proponents want to change that. The Lindesmith Center and the San Francisco Medical Society held a "Just Say Know" conference in San Francisco [in October 1999] to initiate the effort to replace "no-use" drug education with "safe-use" programs in schools.

The Lindesmith Center is part of billionaire George Soros' Open Society Institute in New York. Soros has funded drug-legalization efforts for a decade. Publicly, proponents deny they want to legalize drugs. They say they just want to "reform" the drug laws. Now they want to reform drug-free education. The Lindesmith Center recommends the book "Chocolate to Morphine: Everything You Need to Know About Mind-Altering Drugs." The book claims there is no such thing as a good or bad drug, just good and bad relationships with drugs. It says we must teach children how to have good relationships with harmful, addictive drugs.

> High levels of drug use among teens . . . produced high levels of drug abuse, drug addiction and drug-related deaths.

The Lindesmith Center introduced its new publication at the conference, called "Safety-First: A Reality-Based Approach to Teens, Drugs, and Drug Education." The pamphlet advises parents to "keep the channels of communication open, find ways to keep the conversation going, and listen, listen, listen."

The pamphlet also tells parents to encourage kids to "be honest" about their drug experiences and that "there must be no negative repercussions for their input and honesty."

Consequences of Drugs

Unfortunately, some hard-working, affluent, church-going parents in Georgia took this advice. Their teenagers did what they wanted with no negative repercussions from mom or dad. Their 12- and 13-year-olds were free to smoke, get drunk, get high and engage in group sex. Nobody told them no.

The kids got syphilis. One died driving home drunk from spring break. Another stabbed a friend. They are called "The Lost Children of Rockdale County," and the TV news show *Frontline* introduced them to us on PBS.

What can parents do? Set limits for your kids. Set consequences if they break your rules. Enforce consequences if rules are broken. Love them enough to be their parents, not their best friends. Be the adults they need to protect them from the world's dangers. And fight to keep "safe use" drug education out of your schools.

Or be prepared to watch a *Frontline* sequel a few years from now on "The Lost Children of America."

Reprinted, with permission, from "'Safe Use' Drug Philosophy Is a Step Backward," by Sue Rusche and Betty Sembler, *San Francisco Chronicle*, November 8, 1999.

Addiction
and Recovery

Recognizing Symptoms of Drug or Alcohol Addiction

Kaiser Permanente

Drug and alcohol use begins with a choice. But while many people take drugs and alcohol without becoming addicted, others feel compelled to continue taking these substances regardless of negative consequences. Determining whether you or someone you know is becoming addicted to drugs can be vitally important, especially since addiction is a treatable condition and help for addicts is available. The following selection lists symptoms of drug and alcohol addiction as well as questions people can ask themselves to determine whether they or someone they know has a problem with alcohol or drugs. It was produced by Kaiser Permanente, the nation's largest nonprofit health maintenance organization.

*D*o you, or someone you love, have a problem with alcohol or drugs?

Teresa likes to drink. "It relaxes me. I look forward to a drink or two at the end of a long day. I don't get really drunk very of-

Excerpted from "Thinking About Alcohol and Drugs," an article in the online library section of the Kaiser Permanente website at www.kaiserpermanente.org/toyourhealth/library/core-alcohol.html. Reprinted with permission.

ten—maybe when I get my check each month, or when a friend stops by, but usually not in the middle of the week. And, I never drink hard liquor—only wine. I don't have a problem."

Jerry takes a tranquilizer when he needs a good night's sleep. "Sometimes I am so wired and have so many things on my mind that I can't get a decent night's sleep. If I have something important to do in the morning, I just can't risk a night without sleep, so I take a tranquilizer to knock me out. Then I know I'll be fresh in the morning. I only do it a few times a month; I wouldn't call that a drug problem."

> Substance abuse is about lack of control.

Michael uses marijuana or cocaine once a week or so. "Actually, the biggest problem I see with using marijuana and cocaine is that it gets to be so expensive. Plus my reflexes aren't what they used to be and my friends tell me I'm not much fun to be around when I'm on them. I try to use them only when I feel like I really have to have more energy to get something done. I don't think I have a drug problem."

Is Teresa an alcoholic? Are Jerry and Michael drug addicts? Maybe they are; maybe they aren't. We don't know for sure. We do know what they use, and we know about how often they use it. But, this doesn't tell us the whole story. Substance abuse isn't only about what a person drinks, smokes, snorts, shoots, or eats.

Substance abuse is about lack of control. It is about feeling that you must take drugs or alcohol even though you know you will suffer negative consequences.

How Does It Happen?

People begin taking and continue to take drugs or alcohol for a lot of reasons. Some of them are listed below:

To feel good	To escape uncomfortable feelings
Loneliness	To relieve depression
Peer pressure	To relieve stress
Boredom	To be uninhibited

But, what happens is that the drug begins taking over the user's life. You lose the ability to choose whether you want to take it without even realizing it. For example, you come home after a tough day, and automatically have a drink, and then another. You can't stop yourself because drinking alcohol just feels right. It has taken control of you. It is not the amount of drugs or alcohol that is as important as the fact that you feel a need to take them. That persistent need, which is so hard to admit, is the heart of the problem.

Unwelcome Effects of Drugs

When someone loses control over the use of drugs or alcohol, it can ruin that person's whole life. Besides the loss of self-respect, the drug-abuser can suffer discomfort, anxiety, disease, mental illness, and even death.

Drug abuse can also cause hardship and pain to family, friends, co-workers, and anyone else nearby. Pregnant women who are abusers produce infants with deformities, brain damage and even AIDS. Parents who are drug/alcohol abusers serve as poor role-models, teaching their children to be irresponsible, violent, suspicious. Marriages, families, and friendships fall apart as problems with money, work, school, and the law mount to unbearable heights. Co-workers shun and bosses fire drug-abusers.

> You might be a drug-abuser and might not even be aware of it.

Recognizing Symptoms of Drug or Alcohol Abuse

Abuse of drugs and alcohol hurts millions of people every day:

- People in all parts of the world
- People with and without jobs
- People with and without families

You might be a drug-abuser and might not even be aware of it. Check the list below to see if the symptoms might apply to you or to someone you know.

Behavior Style

❏ Arrogant
❏ Argumentative
❏ Absent-minded
❏ Secretive
❏ Explosive anger
❏ Unexplained absences
❏ Doing dangerous things
❏ Accident prone
❏ Borrowing money from friends

Body

❏ Exhaustion
❏ Sloppy appearance
❏ Blank stare
❏ Bloodshot eyes
❏ Puffy face
❏ Slurred speech
❏ Unsteady walk
❏ Low energy
❏ Frequent illnesses

Feelings

❏ Depression
❏ Anxiety
❏ Irritability
❏ Suspicion
❏ Mood swings
❏ Withdrawal

Work Patterns

❏ Frequent mistakes
❏ Uneven productivity
❏ Decreased motivation
❏ Carelessness
❏ Lapses of memory
❏ Difficulty with complex tasks

Is This You?

Here are some questions that have helped many people take a close look at their own use of alcohol and other drugs. Answer them by circling the "Y" for "yes" or "N" for "no."

Y   N   Have you ever felt the need or tried to cut down on your alcohol/drug intake?

Y   N   Do you test yourself for control, say you won't take drugs, and then take them anyway?

Y   N   Do you think it would be difficult to enjoy life if you could not take another drink or drug?

Y   N   Do you use alcohol or other drugs as a way of handling stressful situations or life problems?

Y   N   Have you ever gotten angry at someone for telling you that you drink/take drugs too much?

Y   N   Have you ever felt guilty about your drinking/drug use?

Y N Have you ever felt like you need a drink/drugs to get you going in the morning?

Y N Do you hide your alcohol/drugs or take them when no one is looking?

Y N Do you take more drinks/drugs than you planned?

Y N Do you have wide swings in mood and personality?

Is This Your Family?

Here are some questions that might apply to you and your family. Answer them as you did above.

Y N Do family members blame themselves for not being able to help you control your drinking/drug-taking?

Y N Do family members feel embarrassed by the way you act?

Y N Do family members avoid social situations, such as inviting friends over, because of your drinking/drug-taking?

Y N Do you use alcohol or other drugs as a way of handling stressful situations or life problems?

Y N Are there unspoken rules in the family about speaking about "the problem"?

Y N Do family members feel fearful or suspicious due to your mood changes, anger, or violence?

If your answer is "yes" to any of . . . [these questions], you might have a problem. But, you can do something about it.

There Is Hope and Plenty of Help

Five years ago, Pamela's life hit rock bottom. After several years of alcohol and cocaine use, she found herself without a job, without a family, without her self-respect, and without a future. Cocaine and alcohol controlled her life. Finally she realized she was in trouble. She got help by calling KPRR, the Kaiser Recovery Program. It's still very hard, but she has taken control of her life. She has a new job. She has friends who will stick with her. And, she likes the person she sees in the mirror each morning.

Pamela is not an unusual miracle story. Every year, thousands of drug users take control of their lives. It's never easy, and it's very hard to do alone, but people do it. They get help. They get better. . . .

Three Steps

There are three steps to managing use of too much alcohol or drugs:

Awareness Become aware of the dangers of alcohol and drug use. Find out what it means to be dependent on or addicted to drugs.

Acceptance Accept that you have a problem. Stop fooling yourself that you can quit any time you want. Denial is your biggest enemy.

> Every year, thousands of drug users take control of their lives.

Action Take action. Decide to do something about your problem by:
- looking for new ways to solve old problems
- changing your habits
- going to a counselor who works with substance abusers . . .

It's Your Choice

Abuse of alcohol or drugs begins with a choice. When you started drinking, smoking, popping, shooting, etc., whether because of peer pressure, boredom, curiosity, or some other reason, you *chose* to use alcohol and/or other drugs. Maybe now it has gotten out of hand, out of control. Maybe it is affecting your life in ways you don't like. Maybe it is affecting those around you in ways you don't want. But the choice is still yours. Even if you need the alcohol or other drugs to feel normal, ask yourself, "Is this the kind of normal life I want for myself and those around me?"

It takes courage and determination to accept that you have a problem and you want to reclaim control of your own life. But you can do it. Help is available. You are worth the effort.

A Teen's Inside View of Drug Addiction

Destiny

Fifteen-year-old Destiny (a pseudonym) tells the story of how she became addicted to drugs. Her own experiences, and those of a close friend, led her to conclude that drugs can take control of people's lives. Destiny is a teen correspondent for WholeFamily.com, a teen and family advice website. Names in the article have been changed to protect privacy.

You've seen them—glassy eyes in sunken eye sockets, pale skin hanging off their bones. If you haven't already guessed, I'm talking about junkies. They messed up at some point in their lives by "experimenting" and got addicted. Now they want you to try some, too. See how it helped us? See how much better we are now? Come on, one hit won't hurt. One smoke won't get you hooked. One little dose won't kill you.

That's the biggest load of crap I've ever heard.

What Drugs Do

Drugs kill. You hear about it almost every day. Heroin overdoses, pot laced with some deadly meth, LSD overdoses causing people to think they are invincible, people dropping acid and

Reprinted, with permission, from "Drug Addiction: An Inside View," by Destiny, an online article at www.aboutteensnow.com/substance_abuse/insider.html. Copyright © 2000 by WholeFamily Center, Inc.; www.wholefamily.com.

then veering off the road because "snakes" were attacking them. You still think drugs seem like the way to go?

Listen up.

My close friend Ralph smokes pot every day. He's also dropped acid, shot up heroin, snorted coke, and done just about any other drug out there, even the designer drugs. He's very lucky that he's not dead. He's been in the hospital quite a few times. He almost OD'd not too long ago.

"LEAVING SO SOON? WHY, THE AGONY'S JUST GETTING STARTED!"

Jim Borgman. Reprinted by special permission of King Features Syndicate. All rights reserved.

Ralph used to be one of those people who say, "I won't get hooked. I'm too strong." Now he feels like he's going crazy if he goes without a smoke every few hours. Do you want to turn out like that? I didn't think so.

You never fully understand what drugs do to you unless you experience it firsthand. But that doesn't mean to go out and try some stuff just to get experienced. I have many friends who are addicted to various things. Unfortunately, I was too dumb to let that tell me not to try drugs.

I got myself addicted to inhalants and pot. I'm still struggling with both of those things. Hearing that is all it takes to prove to some people that drugs are the wrong way to go. Other people, it does take a personal experience for this to be driven home.

Getting Hooked

Every single drug out there is addictive. You may have to take it more than once, but you will get hooked. Pretty soon, you have to start taking larger doses to get the same high as your first time. Later on, you need to take huge doses just to stay normal, not to mention to get high. You end up investing hundreds—more likely thousands—of dollars to keep up with yourself. Eventually, you try other drugs to see if you can get a better high. Then, to make more money, you start dealing.

It's really amazing how many different people buy. Men in business suits, pregnant teens, ten-year-old runaways, old men and women looking for a last thrill of life. Does that sound like a good thing to get into? Would you feel good selling crack to a little boy with a tear-stained face and dried blood on his lip? Would

> No matter how hard it gets, . . . drugs will make it worse.

you feel good seeing babies born as heroin-addicts, because you sold to their mothers while they were pregnant? Would you feel good if one day you were selling a person some very strong LSD, and your mother drove by and saw you? Would you feel good if you had to spend the rest of your life in rehab, rather than indulge in your old dreams of owning a law firm?

Just remember this one thing, if nothing else: No matter how hard it gets, no matter how bad it may seem, drugs will make it worse.

Life in a Drug Abuse Treatment Center

Mike S.

For many teens, recovering from drug addiction means a stay in a residential treatment center. Recovering drug addicts live away from their families in structured and drug-free environments for periods ranging from one month to more than a year, where they receive various forms of individual and group counseling. The following article by teen writer Mike S. briefly describes what life is like for teens in drug treatment. It notes that a key element is detailed rules circumscribing all aspects of participants' lives. The article is taken from the website of the Partnership for a Drug-Free America, a coalition of advertising and media professionals who produce antidrug ads and drug education materials.

"When I first found out I was going to [a treatment center], I thought I was lucky," says Patti. "I thought it was a good excuse for me to get out of school and get my mom away from me. I had no idea that there were going to be any rules. I just thought I was going to come here nine hours a day and like, watch TV and have stupid groups and then go home."

That's what Patti thought six months ago. Now the 15-year-

Reprinted, with permission, from "Learning to Live by the Rules: Teens in Drug Treatment," by Mike S., published on the website of Partnership for a Drug-Free America at www.drugfreeamerica.org, under the "kids and teens" section.

old knows that the "stupid groups" are a huge amount of work, that TV is not a big part of a treatment day, and that even when she goes home for the night, she can't leave the rules behind.

Tough Rules

Although no two drug treatment programs are exactly alike, they all have one thing in common: rules. Think your current house and school rules are tough? Add these to your list:

- You have to attend several more hours than regular school—or you might even have to live there.
- You don't have the freedom to run down to the store or even use the restroom whenever you feel like it. You have to earn the right to go places on your own.
- You have to work a full-time job within the center—and it usually starts out with cleaning floors or scrubbing bathrooms.
- You have to sign in and out every single day. Somebody always has to know where you are.
- You can't see your old friends.
- You have to write a detailed plan of how you'll spend your weekend—and stick to it.

Now you see a bit more of what kids in drug treatment programs have to face.

Of course, these rules all have their reasons. And although it may take some time, many kids who end up in drug treatment centers learn how rules work for them and make their lives better.

"When you're out there using [you think] we have to do it our way," says 17-year-old Samantha. "They get us out of that mode where it has to be our way. You can get the same result—and it may actually be easier."

Daily Life

Structure is key in a treatment center. "I ran this place every day for four months. I was in charge—senior coordinator," says 17-

year-old Mike. "We have a set structure everyday." The day includes a morning meeting—with an 8:30 a.m. kickoff, school, intense group sessions to work on a variety of drug- and life-related issues, and time for jobs.

> Although no two drug treatment programs are exactly alike, they all have one thing in common: rules.

The harder the kids work during groups and at their jobs, the faster they gain back the privileges that they once took for granted. "When they let you go off the property the first time it's like the best feeling," says Mike. "The first time you go is so great cause you had no privileges for three or four months and nobody trusted you for three or four months and then you walk down the block. You feel great."

Break the rules and privileges are taken away. "I basically followed all the rules but I slipped up toward the end—I get to a mode where I don't care or I feel like I'm not going nowhere with this then I'm like, forget it and I just act out all around," says 16-year-old Anthony. "That only happened for about a week [and] I didn't go into the [next] part of the treatment. That kind of knocked into me. I'm working on it so that in September I go into the [next] part of the treatment and I don't have to be told when and where I can go to the bathroom."

The Payoff

Of course, the rewards for all the work go far beyond bathroom privileges or a trip to the local store: "The best thing about this place is that after you've been here a while, you can actually look back at your past and at your present and go, 'god my life is so much better now.' You can see everything that you have, everything right out in front of you, and everything that you lost from back when," says Mike. "You can see you have so much and your life is going to be so great and you can do so much."

One Teen's Story of Addiction and Recovery

Rachel

Rachel battled drug and alcohol addiction for several years before successfully becoming clean and sober. The key to her recovery was a special alternative high school for recovering drug and alcohol addicts. In the following excerpt from testimony she gave before a Congressional committee, she tells how she got started on drugs, her struggles with addiction, and her ongoing recovery.

I got into drugs and alcohol at a very young age. I have an older brother, and when I was a kid he was going through a whole bunch of problems with depression and drug abuse. Because of this, my parents had to give him lots of attention, and I was not paid attention to very much. At that time, I swore to myself that I would NEVER do drugs.

Problems with Drugs

But later on, as my respect and love for my brother grew, I started using drugs so I could fit in with his friends and be a cool sister. But it didn't stop there. I started to use more on my own, and I became depressed. My parents sent me to a girl's boarding school for the ninth and tenth grades. My ninth grade year went

Reprinted from Rachel's testimony before the U.S. Senate Committee on the Judiciary hearing on "Drug Abuse Among Our Children: A Growing National Crisis," June 17, 1998.

pretty well. I was in all honors classes and my grades were good. But in tenth grade I discovered that by smoking marijuana I could escape from all the pressure and depression that I was going through. So I started to smoke it every day, all day. But that wasn't enough. I discovered LSD, cocaine, PCP, and other drugs, and found that they worked just as well, if not better, and I thought they were fun. So I used anything that I could get my hands on.

Eventually I got kicked out of that school, and came back to live with my parents. During the time that I was at the boarding school I was in four rehabilitation facilities and ended up in the hospital for dehydration. I was 20 pounds lighter than I am now. I guess I just didn't care about anything except drugs, including eating or drinking. When I came home my drug abuse continued to get worse. I started to drink alcohol more because it was more available.

I ended up detoxing at Bethesda Navy Hospital, but once I got out, I still didn't stop. My parents didn't trust me at all, I hated myself, and I had no friends that liked me for who I was. They only liked me for the drugs I had.

> I knew I couldn't stop on my own.

My psychiatrist refused to give me any more anti-depressants until I went to another rehabilitation center. So I went, and there, for the first time, considered the possibility of getting clean. I was able to do it for three weeks, but ended up relapsing.

A Special Program

I knew I couldn't stop on my own. The school that I was supposed to be attending . . . wasn't working out, there were so many drugs there, and everybody knew me as a drug addict. But luckily . . . [there was] an alternative program called the Phoenix I school that is specifically for kids who need to get into recovery for drug and alcohol addiction.

They accepted me with open arms. Through Phoenix I was introduced to 12-step programs, and I had to get a sponsor (someone to guide me through the 12 steps and help me with any problem that I had). They also encouraged me to stay clean through an ongoing urinalysis.

That was the first time that I had a clean and sober peer group that knew what I was going through. We were all there to help each other. I was able to stay sober, and my grades improved tremendously. I had a great attendance record, when before I was skipping school as often as I could.

Through group therapy at Phoenix, I developed skills that I had never had. I learned how to communicate with people in healthy ways, give and accept constructive criticism, and just work on myself.

I got on the honor roll, and got straight A's for the first time in my life. I began to like the person I was becoming. My parents started to trust me again, and I developed a great relationship with them. I have two extremely close friends that I am able to communicate with, and they like me for who I am. My parents are even letting me drive their car.

Clean and Sober

At this point I have 8 and 1/2 months clean and sober. I've learned that there are so many kids out there who are using drugs that don't have any way of getting help. It would really be great if there were other recovery high schools in other public school systems so that other addicted kids could get the help they so desperately need. Most kids don't know that the temporary elevation from the pain through drugs is just not worth the long-term consequences; they don't have anyone to open their eyes. I was just extremely lucky that I had a place to go in my school system, otherwise I don't know how I would have gotten clean in the first place.

What Should You Do If a Friend Has a Drug or Alcohol Problem?

DrugHelp.org

Even if you never take or become addicted to drugs, substance abuse can affect your life through friends or family members. Teens face choices not only on whether to take drugs themselves, but also on how to deal with others who may have a drug or alcohol problem. The following article argues for reaching out to help even though it might seem "pushy" and includes advice on how to talk with friends who are struggling with drugs and alcohol. It was produced by DrugHelp.org, an online drug treatment referral center created by Phoenix House, a drug abuse treatment organization.

D rug and alcohol addictions are not just phases or bad habits that will go away. If left untreated, chemical dependency is as deadly as cancer.

When someone has a drug problem, it's not always easy to know what to do. Should you talk to them? Should you leave them alone? Should you get someone else to help?

Think about it this way. If you saw someone having a heart at-

Reprinted, with permission, from "If Your Friend Has a Drug or Alcohol Problem . . ." an online article published at www.drughelp.org/intervention/friend.

tack, you'd call an ambulance. If they were depressed, you'd listen to their problems. If they wanted to hurt themselves, you would try to stop them. You'd be there for them. That's what being a friend is about.

Helping Your Friends

Some of my friends started using drugs recreationally, but after a while, their relationship with me changed.

They treated me badly and ignored me. They seemed like strangers and we didn't know what to talk about anymore. But I knew the drugs were talking, so I just felt sad.

I wanted to help them, but I was afraid that if I stuck my nose in their business, I'd lose them. Still, sometimes I wondered if I should be more of a bully and tell them to talk to me about their problems.

I think friends should help each other, so I went to Stan Adamson, a drug counselor . . . to see if he had any ideas how to do it.

Mr. Adamson suggested you might first try talking with your friends about ways they've changed. You might say they seem very stressed or upset all the time, and see where the conversation goes from there.

But he also said it was OK to be more straight forward and let your friends know that you think they have a problem with drugs. . . .

If your friends don't want help, you can't force them to get it. I don't think people should feel guilty if they can't help their friends, which is how I used to feel.

But I do believe that the wrong thing to do is to pretend that you think what your friends are doing is cool when actually they are in trouble. This only helps your friends ignore their problems even longer.

Edith Littuan, *New Youth Connections*, March 1998.

But it's hard being a friend to someone who breaks promises, forgets to call, borrows money and never pays it back, and gets "high" instead of spending time with you like they used to.

You might never know it, but your friend needs you now more than ever.

Common Fears About Getting Involved

You know your friend needs help, but every time you decide to talk to them something holds you back.

Maybe you don't want to "butt in" or you're afraid they'll think you're being pushy or "uncool."

If your friend were suicidal, and no one "butted in," what would happen? They might end up in an emergency room, or worse. The same goes for someone who's abusing drugs or alcohol; the problem is just as dangerous and getting help just as critical.

Substance abuse is one of the leading causes of death in this country. Talking to your friend may save their life.

Do you think that your friend will get mad and you'll lose the friendship?

It's never easy to talk to someone about their problems. Sometimes the person feels ashamed, guilty, and, yes, angry.

Don't let a negative reaction throw you off. Prepare for it. Remember that drug abuse causes many different kinds of behavior, including anger and denial. Concentrate on your goal; to bring the issue out into the open. Let your friend know you want to help and you're there for them. You may be surprised to find that your friend wanted someone to help all along.

> It's never easy to talk to someone about their problems.

Before approaching someone about their problem, get professional advice. Talk to a school counselor, an Employee Assistance Program, a teacher, doctor, nurse, parent, or someone in your church or synagogue. Keep the conversation private and confidential; talk in general terms about the problem and ask for advice. It will help you figure out what steps to take.

Talking with Your Friend

When, where?

Make sure the timing is right. Talk to your friend when they're sober and clear-headed like in the morning before school or work. You won't get anywhere talking to them when they are drunk, high, or coming down.

Try talking to your friend the day after they've been drinking or using drugs and they are feeling hung over, guilty, and the experience is still fresh. Remember that you're not addressing just one incident, but a pattern of behavior; so it's O.K. if you can't talk to them right away.

Meet in a neutral place; a coffee shop, park, or some other public place. Make sure alcohol is not available.

If you know someone who you trust, a counselor, someone from Narcotics Anonymous (NA) or Alcoholics Anonymous (AA), or another concerned friend or family member, you might try to enlist their help as well. Just make sure they are well prepared too.

How?

- Always use a gentle, caring tone of voice; you're talking to them as a friend, not out of pity.
- Try not to judge. Don't start out by accusing your friend of being a drug addict or an alcoholic. This will only put them on the defensive and they might walk away.
- Tell them how you feel; how worried you are and how you feel when you see them drunk or high. Express your concern.
- Tell your friend about the things you've seen them do when they're drunk or high. Use specific examples, and tell them you want to help.
- Be prepared for anger, denial, and even rejection. Your friend may claim they don't have a problem and may get an-

gry. This is a common reaction for people using drugs or alcohol. Don't take it personally; remember the person your friend really is and focus on the problem, not their attitude.

- Be prepared with information on where to get help. Offer to go with your friend to a meeting or take them for an assessment. This will show you really care and are willing to spend your own time and energy to get them the help they need. But only offer if you're ready to follow through.

If your friend has a serious problem and you can't convince them to get help on their own, you should consider talking to their parents, a teacher, or someone else in a position of authority. The consequences of not getting help are too dangerous to ignore.

Accepting that there's a problem and asking for help can be scary and very difficult. Your friend will have to face the pain they've caused themselves and other people in their life. This is often an upsetting and painful process. But until they can see the damage done by drug or alcohol use and the loss of real friends, happiness, and self-respect it's caused, they will not be committed to changing their life.

> Your concern and support might be just what's needed to help your friend turn their life around.

When your friend is ready, you can offer them information about places in their area to go for help. Take the time before your "talk" to find out what's available where your friend lives. Make a list of phone numbers, meeting places, and meeting times for local counseling services and treatment programs.

The Road to Recovery

Whether your friend succeeds in recovery or not, you should feel good about your decision to help them. The most important thing is for you and your friend to *do something*. Every attempt at help is an opportunity for recovery, and it's never too late to start.

As your friend begins the process of recovery, they will go

through many difficult changes. They'll need to spend a lot of time at support groups, in counseling, and building friendships with other people in recovery. You might wonder if they still care about you and appreciate your help. This is a normal and important part of recovery, but it can be painful. You might feel like you've lost the friend you went out of your way to help. But most people in recovery return to their old friends with a lot more to give than before. Be patient and give your friend room to grow.

A Final Note

No matter how much you care and how hard you try, ultimately it's up to your friend to get help. The decision to stop using drugs or alcohol must come from them. They have to want it for themselves and it is their commitment that will carry them through the difficult times ahead. You are not responsible for your friend's success or failure at recovery. All you can do is talk to them, show how much you care, and encourage them to get help. Your concern and support might be just what's needed to help your friend turn their life around.

Chapter 5

Making Decisions
About Drugs and
Your Life

Saying No to Your Friends

Erin Donovan

Many teens may not want to experiment with drugs, but find it difficult to say no to their friends or to resist the temptation to try drugs just one time. One teen wrote to the advice website WholeFamily.com asking how to deal with such a situation; the following exchange consists of that person's question and the response by Erin Donovan, senior teen advisor at WholeFamily.com. Donovan, a 1999 high school graduate, urges the questioner to be true to his/her beliefs on whether to take drugs. Trying drugs just because one's friends are doing it is a poor reason for risking one's health and well-being, she argues.

Q: Hey! I read what your [web]site said about drugs. And I think that they are stupid. But that is not going to stop people from doing them. I have a group of friends that do them. And they seem fine. They want me to try them. Everyone does them. They can't be that bad. I mean if I try them only once it isn't gonna matter, right? Plus, how could I say no to my friends?

A: People do drugs regardless of all the advice and research out there about how they will destroy your life. At this time in

Reprinted, with permission, from "Dealing with Drugs," by Erin Donovan, an on-line article at www.aboutteensnow.com/advice/erin/q_and_a.html. Copyright 2000 by WholeFamily Center Inc.; www.wholefamily.com.

our lives it starts out as just wanting to have a good time, or see what all the buzz is about, but ask any crack addict, alcoholic, cocaine addict, etc. . . . if they had one line of advice to give what would it be, and they almost always answer with "Don't even try it. Don't ever start."

Reprinted from The Luann Health Series, by Greg Evans; © GEC Inc. Reprinted by permission of United Features Syndicate, Inc.

No one takes a hit off a joint expecting to get hooked on crack or other drugs; it's just marijuana, right? But that's the first step on the steep trek to rock bottom. Especially since it's very common now for marijuana to be laced with other drugs. People like to mix cocaine or PCP in with the marijuana, and most of the time you won't realize it's in there until you've already smoked it.

You may think that your friends doing drugs seem fine, but drugs lead to serious problems—with school, parents, society, the law, work and other friends who don't use. The problems start to build up, and continue to grow. People get out of touch with themselves emotionally, and wind up being numb most of the time, not able to cope, and then instead of using drugs to feel good anymore, people use them to feel less bad.

And not everyone does them, though it can start to seem like that when your group of friends starts. When you start using the excuse that "everyone" does something, then the cliche comes up "If all your friends jumped off a bridge would you do it?" You are an individual, you are responsible for your own actions, your own outcomes. I hate that cliche that I quoted above, but it leads to this answer: "If all my friends were to jump off a bridge, I wouldn't jump with them, but instead go catch them at the bottom."

And that's what you should be thinking about. You don't have to stop being friends with them, but don't put yourself in positions where people are going to be trying to get you to jump off bridges either.

Tell them you're just not into the drug scene. You may have to ease off the friendship for awhile until they come to

> You are responsible for your own actions.

their senses, find some new friends, or be strong enough to realize that you don't want to be a part of the drug thing, and don't let anyone tear you from your values when you are with them.

Self-Esteem

That is where self-esteem comes from. Sticking to what you believe in, and not letting anyone talk you into betraying yourself. Never betray yourself. When you are around them keep firmly in mind what you want out of your life, and that jail cells and crack alleys are not the roads that take you there.

Every time they offer you drugs, just look them straight in the eye and say "No thank you, I'm not into that." Say it again, and again until they stop asking.

You seem like an intelligent person, and I'm sure you'll find the strength to stay true to yourself.

Wanting to Quit

Go Ask Alice!

What should people do if they already take drugs such as marijuana on a regular basis, but now desire to quit? An anonymous teen posed this question to the "Go Ask Alice!" health question and answer internet service website produced by Columbia University's Health Education Program, on which university educators and health care providers answer queries on drugs, sexuality, and other matters. In this instance, "Alice" responds by discussing the problem of psychological dependence and by suggesting that the student talk about their situation with a counselor, a trusted friend or family member, or a self-help group such as Marijuana Anonymous.

D ear Alice,
   I have been doing weed for about six months now and on occasion a few other drugs. I usually do it only on average three times a week and a lot more on the weekends. I feel that it is ruining my life because my concentration is terrible and my marks have dropped significantly (20 points). I feel like I'm in a dream all the time and it just isn't fun anymore. I have heard that pot is not addictive but I have tried to stop but I feel sick and irritable if I don't smoke up. I have realized I need to quit but I

Reprinted, with permission, from "Wants to Stop Smoking Pot," a letter sent to Go Ask Alice!® Columbia University's Health Education Program, published at www.goaskalice.columbia.edu/1579.html. Copyright © 1999 by The Trustees of Columbia University.

can't. Why can't I stop if this "soft drug" is not addictive? Am I crazy? Please help. I want my life back. Thank you so much.

Permafried

Dear Permafried,

Current research tells a conflicting story about marijuana and addiction. On the one hand, pot does not appear to cause physical dependence or any of the severe physical withdrawal symptoms associated with other drugs, like cocaine or heroin. However, it may cause a psychological dependence, characterized by a sense of needing the drug, and the sensations it produces, in order to function "normally." In this case, the feelings you describe could be the result of a psychological withdrawal.

Common Symptoms

You said that you felt sick and irritable if you don't smoke up. These symptoms have definitely been seen before in people using pot heavily, which you are. They can result from the pot alone or from pot that's cut with other substances unknown to you. When trying to cut down or stop smoking, some people feel tired all the time, have headaches and rapid mood changes, and feel depressed or anxious. When some heavy pot users try to stop, they experience nervousness, insomnia, a loss of appetite and weight loss, chills, tremors, depression, and/or mental confusion.

> One thing to consider is whether you find yourself continuing to use pot despite negative . . . consequences.

Over time, heavy users may also note difficulty with short-term memory, impaired abstract thinking, a lack of interest in their usual social activities, and less motivation, some of which it sounds like you're experiencing. You might want to think about how the other drugs you're taking have affected you physically and mentally as well.

When addicted to a drug, a person usually thinks a lot about getting and using the drug, and will have trouble staying off when attempting to quit, which you mention. One thing to consider is whether you find yourself continuing to use pot despite negative physical, emotional, or social consequences. You might also ponder whether wanting or using pot controls your behavior.

Talk It Over

You've mentioned that you find yourself continuing to use marijuana despite the fact that it no longer brings you pleasure. Recognizing this and looking for help quitting are two very important steps—which you've already taken. Talking with a counselor or health care provider might be a next step. There are many professionals who specialize in this area. . . . There are also many chapters of Marijuana Anonymous, a self-help group modeled after the design of other twelve-step programs. . . .

You might also want to talk with a trusted friend or family member about how you've been feeling and your need for his or her support. Talking with your dean or an academic advisor about the situation, even without specifics, can help you re-focus on your educational goals and get your studies back on track.

How to Become Chemically Independent

Jim Parker

Once a former user makes the decision to quit taking drugs, the challenge remains how to cope and thrive without relying on mind-altering chemicals. Jim Parker, a writer for a drug abuse education organization, describes some basic steps people can take to live drug-free. These include getting adequate nutrition and sleep, coping with stress, and finding new activities.

What goes up must come down. It's a basic law of physics. We call it gravity, but the principle extends further than simply explaining why apples fall down.

It also describes what happens to people when they pump themselves up with chemicals: Eventually, they come down, too.

It's the First Law of Chemical Consciousness—the old rebound principle. And it holds true no matter what your favorite psychoactive substance is—or used to be. Coffee or cocaine, alcohol or LSD, sooner or later you come down.

And when you do, you'll notice that the First Law has a corollary: The higher you go, the further you fall. That means that once you do come down, you usually end up lower than when you started.

Reprinted, with permission, from "Cleaning Yourself Up: A Guide to Getting Your Head (and Heart, Body, and Soul) Together for People Who Are Becoming Chemically Dependent," by Jim Parker, an online article at www.doitnow.org/pages/135.html. Copyright © 2000 by DIN Publications/Do It Now Foundation. All rights reserved.

What do you do about it after the fact? Well, a first impulse may be to use more of the chemical you started with (or even a different one) to get back up (or down) to where you started from. That's one option.

Of course, that ultimately leaves you even further down—or further up (or off) the wall, if you've been climbing one lately.

The other option is to stop the cycle completely. It's trickier, since it involves effort and patience on your part and requires putting up with feeling down long enough to let your body re-center itself. But it can be done.

That's where we come in.

In this article, we'll talk about ways of breaking out of the chemical-dependency trap and discuss techniques that can make the withdrawal process easier on your body and mind.

Because even though time is a factor in freeing yourself from chemicals, a lot can be done to cut that time to a minimum, and get you back on your feet again—one day and one step at a time.

Body/Mind 101

Mind and body are inseparable parts of the same basic unit; what happens to one automatically affects the other.

That means that getting back to where you want to be will require paying attention to the needs of both.

Once you've gotten over your immediate reliance on drugs and/or alcohol (and you really do have to begin there), start with a general cleaning-up program, like the one outlined below.

It's designed to give your body what it really needs—exercise, nutrition, and rest—rather than the chemical substitutes you've been using as your personal gun, whip, and chair.

Nutrition

Poor nutrition doesn't just cause poor physical health. Moodiness, irritability, restlessness, fatigue, and many other "emotional" problems are often directly linked to poor nutrition.

So if you're not eating well, all you're eating is calories—and potential problems.

But what does "eating well" mean? It means eating the same stuff that your mom probably tried to get you to eat a long time ago: Veggies and fresh fruits and grains.

While you're at it, you might want to avoid heavily-processed foods and anything that contains ingredients you can't pronounce or spell, like polysorbate-60 or calcium disodium edta (whatever that is).

Also, cut back on caffeine and sugar, since they're both almost guaranteed to kick in cravings for whatever you're trying to clear out of your system.

> Give your body what it really needs—exercise, nutrition, and rest—rather than . . . chemical substitutes.

Since chemical use tends to deplete vitamins and minerals in the body (especially the B vitamins), supplements are also a great idea.

It's a tricky subject, though, since all vitamins aren't the same. Some—like vitamin C and the B-complex vitamins—are water-soluble, so your body only uses what it needs and excretes the rest.

Other vitamins, though, are fat-soluble (such as A, D and E), and can build up to harmful levels in the body.

If you want to know more, contact a nutritionist or ask someone knowledgeable at a local health-food store.

Remember, though: Everyone has an opinion about nutrition, and what works for someone else (alfalfa sprouts on carob-chip Tofuti?) may not work for you.

So listen to your body. And if you don't feel your absolute best (both physically and mentally), listen some more. There's still room for improvement.

Sleep

Good-old, made-in-the-shade sleep is another key element in any body-cleansing program.

There's just no substitute for the rest and revitalization that sleep can provide. It'll help you adjust psychologically to the changes you're going through and reduce feelings of burnout in the bargain.

So if you really want to be responsible for yourself—and you're serious about staying off whatever you've been on—start giving your body the natural sleep it needs.

If insomnia's a problem—and it often is for cleaning-yourself-up people—check out the section on exercise [see sidebar 1].

Here's why: Sleep disturbances become a lot less of a problem for people who are committed to doing whatever it takes to handle them. You'll be surprised, for example, at how easy it is

Sidebar 1: Running from Problems

Along with proper nutrition, exercise does a lot to tone the body and tune the spirit.

Because not only does sustained activity improve physical fitness, it also triggers a surge in the body's production of endorphins, the chemical messengers that act in the brain to increase positive feelings and reduce stress.

You might have heard about endorphins as the basis for the so-called "runner's high."

It's not hype. Runners do report an expanded sense of well-being after a run.

But increased endorphin levels have been linked to activities other than running. In fact, recent research shows that any intense physical exercise can trigger the same response.

That means that swimming, walking, or almost anything else that gets the heart thumping and the muscles pumping can inspire a major uplift in mood and outlook.

Try it—even if you don't really feel like it.

After all, you've been doing what you feel like all along.

And look where it's got you.

to fall asleep once you commit yourself to a serious jogging or aerobics program.

And besides, what self-respecting ex-dope fiend or alcoholic would want to waste all those free endorphins?

Body/Mind 201

The second step in recovery involves "re-centering" the mind and emotions to break the habits that contributed to your dependency.

This process can involve taking up almost anything from meditation to mah-jong, but it ultimately requires breaking habits of the past that have kept you from fully enjoying the present without a chemical crutch.

As you've realized by now, chemicals don't "solve" problems. What they do is insulate us from problems—which may feel nice for a while, but which rarely resolves anything. By managing problems with chemicals we forget other, more effective ways of dealing with them.

> As you've realized by now, chemicals don't "solve" problems.

Now, you're going to have to teach yourself all over again. And the best—and possibly the most all-encompassing—place to start is learning to manage stress.

Stress

One of the biggest reasons any of us ever had for self-medicating with drugs and alcohol is something we all still have to deal with: simple tension.

It's usually one of the biggest pieces of excess baggage that recovering people carry around, and something each of us needs to unpack in one way or another, sooner or later.

The big question for most newly clean-and-sober people is this: How do you start unstressing when you're an expert at disstressing?

For starters, you need to learn to identify tension and beat it to the punch. Then, if you've gotten used to clobbering it with something pharmacological (say, a six-pack or a joint after work), find a new way.

You might try something as simple as taking a shower, for example, or learn a meditation technique.

Don't know any? Then check out [sidebar 2]. It describes a

Sidebar 2: The 15-Minute Meditator

One of the most up-to-the-minute methods for beating stress happens to be one of the oldest. It's meditation, and in recent years, it's been dusted off and demystified and studied in depth by researchers, who consider it one of the best tools for managing everyday tension and anxiety.

Learning to meditate has never been easier, either. One researcher, Herbert W. Benson of the Harvard Medical School, offers an introduction to the basic elements of meditation in his book, *The Relaxation Response.* According to Dr. Benson, all you need to do is follow these main points:

1. Find a quiet place where you won't be disturbed for 15 minutes or so.
2. Close your eyes and relax all the muscles in your body.
3. Focus your attention on your breathing, and silently repeat the word "one" (or another single-syllable word, such as "calm") each time you exhale.
4. When thoughts intrude, simply return your focus to the word "one" as you exhale.

Don't push. The goal is to temporarily turn off the flood of thoughts, judgments, and interpretations that flow through our minds. And while that's the goal, don't realistically expect to do it for more than a few seconds at a time any time soon.

Still, if you try it, stick with it. Benson recommends a twice-a-day schedule (mornings and early evenings work best for most people) if you want to get good at it—and get the full range of physical and psychological benefits linked to it.

stripped-down, no-frills approach to meditation that answers another age-old question about the mind: How do you turn the damn thing off?

Just remember—the ability to cool yourself out psycho-emotionally (whether through meditation or not) is like everything else: Practice makes perfect.

New Directions

If you're newly drug-free, we have good news and bad news about your life: It's yours again. Now, all you have to do is make it worth living.

How? The details are up to you, but it's probably going to involve change, and it might not be fast or easy. But, it is worth it.

Because even though change can look more threatening than the everyday grind (no matter how monotonous and frustrating the everyday grind may seem sometimes), it's part of life.

And if you stop and think about it, you may realize that the best, most exciting, most gratifying fun times in your life involved the most change—and often, serious change.

So go out and try something new—aerobics or aikido, web-surfing or white-water rafting—whatever looks like it may help you connect with the future you want to live.

If you look hard enough, you'll see alternatives to an unhappy, stuck, chemically-dependent life everywhere.

In case you'd forgotten, you're a unique person who's perfectly designed to go out into the world and discover what you need—and what needs doing.

Now all you have to do is go out there and do it.

A Mother's Advice to Her Son

Marsha Rosenbaum

Marsha Rosenbaum is a drug policy researcher and head of the San Francisco office of the Lindesmith Center, a research institute that analyzes American approaches to drug prohibition, treatment, and education. She is also the mother of a teen son, to whom she wrote the following letter that was published in the *San Francisco Chronicle.* Rosenbaum argues that although many good reasons exist for teens to avoid drugs or alcohol, many may nonetheless choose to experiment. She urges her son to take the following precautions if he does decide to try drugs: recognize the potential dangers, learn as much as he can, and use moderation and common sense.

Dear Johnny,

This fall you will be entering high school, and like most American teenagers, you'll have to navigate drugs. As most parents, I would prefer that you not use drugs. However, I realize that despite my wishes, you might experiment.

I will not use scare tactics to deter you. Instead, having spent the past 25 years researching drug use, abuse and policy, I will tell

Excerpted from "A Mother's Advice," in *Safety First: A Reality-Based Approach to Teens, Drugs, and Drug Education*, by Marsha Rosenbaum (New York: Lindesmith Center, 1999). Copyright © 1999 The Lindesmith Center. Reprinted by permission of the publisher.

being caught are huge. Here in the United States, the number of arrests for possession of marijuana has more than doubled in the past six years. Adults are serious about "zero tolerance." If caught, you could be arrested, expelled from school, barred from playing sports, lose your driver's license, denied a college loan, and/or rejected for college.

> If you are offered drugs, be cautious.

Despite my advice to abstain, you may one day choose to experiment. I will say again that this is not a good idea, *but if you do,* I urge you to learn as much as you can, and use common sense. There are many excellent books and references, including the Internet, that give you credible information about drugs. You can, of course, always talk to me. If I don't know the answers to your questions, I will try to help you find them.

Use Caution and Moderation

If you are offered drugs, be cautious. Watch how people behave, but understand that everyone responds differently even to the same substance. If you do decide to experiment, be sure you are surrounded by people you can count upon. Plan your transportation and under no circumstances drive or get into a car with anyone else who has been using alcohol or other drugs. Call us or any of our close friends any time, day or night, and we will pick you up, no questions asked and no consequences.

And please, Johnny, use moderation. It is impossible to know what is contained in illegal drugs because they are not regulated. The majority of fatal overdoses occur because young people do not know the strength of the drugs they consume, or how they combine with other drugs. Please do not participate in drinking contests, which have killed too many young people. Whereas marijuana by itself is not fatal, too much can cause you to become disoriented and sometimes paranoid. And of course, smoking can hurt your lungs, later in life and now.

Johnny, as your father and I have always told you about a range of activities (including sex), think about the consequences of your actions before you act. Drugs are no different. Be skeptical and most of all, be safe.

Love,

Mom

Bibliography

Books

Gilda Berger — *Meg's Story: Straight Talk About Drugs.* Brookfield, CT: Millbrook, 1994.

Glenn Alan Cheney — *Drugs, Teens, and Recovery: Real-Life Stories of Trying to Stay Clean.* New York: Enslow, 1993.

Joel Engel — *Addicted: Kids Talking About Drugs in Their Own Words.* New York: Tom Doherty Associates, 1989.

John Hicks — *Drug Addiction: No Way I'm an Addict.* Brookfield, CT: Millbrook, 1997.

Raymond M. Jamiolkowski — *Drugs and Domestic Violence.* New York: Rosen, 1996.

Wendy Klein — *Drugs and Denial.* New York: Rosen, 1998.

Cynthia Kuhn et al. — *Buzzed: The Straight Facts About the Most Used and Abused Drugs from Alcohol to Ecstasy.* New York: W.W. Norton, 1998.

Glenn A. Levant — *Keeping Kids Drug Free: D.A.R.E. Official Parent's Guide.* San Diego: Thunder Bay Press, 1998.

Wendy Maas — *Teen Drug Abuse.* San Diego: Lucent Books, 1998.

Lynn Phillips — *Drug Abuse.* New York: Marshall Cavendish, 1994.

Elizabeth A. Ryan — *Straight Talk About Drugs and Alcohol.* New York: Facts On File, 1995.

Marc A. Schuckit — *Educating Yourself About Alcohol and Drugs: A People's Primer.* New York: Plenum Press, 1998.

Laura Stamper — *When the Drug War Hits Home: Healing the Family Torn by Teenage Drug Abuse.* Minneapolis: Fairview Press, 1997.

Gail B. Stewart — *Teen Addicts.* San Diego: Lucent Books, 2000.

Periodicals

Janice Arenofsky — "The Dangers of Designer Drugs," *Current Health 2,* January 2000.

Anita Bartholomew — "Keeping a Child's Spirit Alive," *Good Housekeeping,* May 1996.

James Bovard — "Unsafe at Any Speed," *American Spectator,* April 1996.

Joseph A. Califano Jr. — "It's All in the Family," *America,* January 15–22, 2000.

Angie Cannon and Carolyn Kleiner — "Teens Get Real," *U.S. News & World Report,* April 17, 2000.

Thomas W. Clark "Keep Marijuana Illegal—for Teens," *Humanist*, May/June 1997.

Henry Pierson Curtis "A Deadly Drug, a New Generation," *Reader's Digest*, July 1998.

Kierna Mayo Dawsey "Blunted," *Essence*, August 1996.

Denise Dowling "Ritalin Alert," *Seventeen*, February 1996.

Gayle Forman "Disturbing Behavior," *Seventeen*, December 1998.

James L. Graff "High Times at New Trier High," *Time*, December 9, 1996.

Linda H. Hamilton "Recreational Drugs: An Alluring Threat to Your Body Chemistry," *Dance Magazine*, January 1996.

Joshua Hammer "The War over Weed," *Newsweek*, March 16, 1998.

Richette L. Haywood "Why More Young People Are Using Drugs," *Jet*, September 9, 1996.

Tricia Hitchcock and Geoff Williams "Help Me, Mom, I'm HOOKED," *Ladies' Home Journal*, February 2000.

Rebecca Lanning "I Was Busted for POT!" *Teen*, June 1996.

Alan I. Leshner "Addiction Is a Brain Disease, and It Matters," *Science*, October 3, 1997.

Daniel R. Levine — "Drugs Are Back—Big Time," *Reader's Digest*, February 1996.

Mike Males and Faye Docuyanan — "The Return of Reefer Madness: Exaggerated Reports of Teenage Drug Use," *Progressive*, May 1996.

Judy Monroe — "Inhalants: Dangerous Highs," *Current Health 2*, September 1995.

Judy Monroe — "Marijuana—a Mind-Altering Drug," *Current Health 2*, March 1998.

Roberta Anne Myers — "Sobriety High," *Seventeen*, February 1995.

Tamar Nordenberg — "The Death of the Party: All the Rave, GHB's Hazards Go Unheeded," *FDA Consumer*, March/April 2000.

Chitra Ragavan and Jeff Glasser — "The Danger of Being Young, Hip, and High," *U.S. News & World Report*, December 13, 1999.

Karen Springen — "Rethinking Zero Tolerance: A Few Schools Are Inching Away from One-Strike Policies," *Newsweek*, February 12, 2001.

Teen — "77 Ways to Say No to Weed and Still Be Cool," June 2000.

Ralph Wood and Linda B. Synovitz — "The Agony of 'Ecstasy,'" *Education Digest*, May 2001.

Scott Wooley

"Greedy Bosses," *Forbes*, August 24, 1998.

Mortimer B.
Zuckerman

"Great Idea for Ruining Kids: The Case for Legalizing Some Drugs Is Seductive—and Completely Wrong," *U.S. News & World Report,* February 24, 1997.

Organizations and Websites

The editors have compiled the following list of organizations and websites concerned with the topics discussed in this book. The descriptions are derived from materials provided by the organizations. All have publications or information available for interested readers. The list was compiled on the date of publication of the present volume; the information provided here may change. Be aware that many organizations take several weeks or longer to respond to inquiries, so allow as much time as possible.

American Council for Drug Education (ACDE)

136 E. 64th St., New York, NY 10163
(800) 488-3784 • fax: (212) 758-6784
e-mail: acde@phoenixhouse.org • website: www.acde.org

The American Council for Drug Education informs the public about the harmful effects of abusing drugs and alcohol. It was created by Phoenix House, the largest private substance abuse treatment program in the United States with residential treatment centers across the country. Among its publications are the Drug Awareness Series of brochures that provide information on illegal drugs.

Drug Enforcement Administration (DEA)

Information Services Section
700 Army Navy Dr., Arlington, VA 22202
(202) 307-1000
website: www.usdoj.gov/dea/

The DEA is the federal agency charged with enforcing the nation's drug laws. It provides information about illegal drugs in its website and in various publications including the books *Get It Straight! The Facts About Drugs* and *Drugs of Abuse.*

Hazelden Foundation
PO Box 11, Center City, MN 55012
(800) 257-7810
website: www.hazelden.org

Hazelden Foundation is a nonprofit organization that provides treatment for alcoholism and drug addiction. It publishes and distributes a wide variety of materials on chemical dependency and recovery.

The Lindesmith Center–Drug Policy Foundation (TLC–DPF)
4455 Connecticut Ave. NW, Suite B-500, Washington, DC 20008-2328
(202) 537-5005 • fax: (202) 537-3007
e-mail: dc@drugpolicy.org • website: www.drugpolicy.org

The foundation is a policy research institute that focuses on broadening the debate on drug policy and related issues. It publishes fact sheets on topics such as drug education and drug prohibition.

Narcotics Anonymous (NA)
PO Box 9999
Van Nuys, CA 91409
(818) 780-3951

NA, comprising more than eighteen thousand groups worldwide, is an organization of recovering drug addicts who meet regularly to help each other abstain from drugs. It publishes the monthlies *NA Way Magazine* and *Newsline.*

National Center on Addiction and Substance Abuse at Columbia University (CASA)

152 W. 57th St., 12th Floor, New York, NY 10019
(212) 841-5200 • fax: (212) 956-8020
website: www.casacolumbia.org

CASA is a private nonprofit organization that works to educate the public about the costs and hazards of substance abuse and the prevention and treatment of all forms of chemical dependency. It produces articles and website publications describing the harmful effects of alcohol and drug addiction and effective ways to address the problem of substance abuse.

National Clearinghouse for Alcohol and Drug Information (NCADI)

PO Box 2345, Rockville, MD 20847-2345
(800) 729-6686 • fax: (301) 468-6433
e-mail: info@health.org • website: www.health.org

The clearinghouse distributes publications of the U.S. Department of Health and Human Services, the National Institute on Drug Abuse, and other federal agencies concerned with alcohol and drug abuse, including the *Substance Abuse Resource Guides* and the newsletter *Prevention Pipeline.*

National Council on Alcoholism and Drug Dependence (NCADD)

12 W. 21st St., 7th Floor, New York, NY 10010
(800) 622-2255 • fax: (212) 645-1690

The National Council on Alcoholism and Drug Dependence works to educate Americans about alcohol and drug abuse. It provides community-based prevention and education programs as well as information and service referrals. The NCADD publishes pamphlets, fact sheets, and other materials that provide statistics on chemical dependency.

National Inhalant Prevention Coalition (NIPC)

2904 Kerbey Ln., Austin, TX 78703

(800) 269-4237 • fax: (512) 477-3932

e-mail: nipc@io.com • website: www.inhalants.org

NIPC serves as an information clearinghouse on inhalant issues. It publishes the booklet *Inhalants: The Silent Epidemic* and provides information on inhalants on its website.

National Institute on Drug Abuse (NIDA)

National Institutes of Health

6001 Executive Blvd., Room 5213, Bethesda, MD 20892

(301) 443-1124

e-mail: information@lists.nida.nih.gov

website:www.nida.nih.gov

NIDA supports and conducts research on drug abuse—including the yearly Monitoring the Future Survey—to improve addiction prevention, treatment, and policy efforts. It publishes the bimonthly *NIDA Notes* newsletter, the periodic *NIDA Capsules* fact sheets, and a catalog of research reports and public education materials such as *Marijuana: Facts for Teens*.

National Organization for the Reform of Marijuana Laws (NORML)

1001 Connecticut Ave. NW, Suite 710, Washington, DC 20036

(202) 483-5500 • fax: (202) 483-0057

e-mail: norml@norml.org • website: www.norml.org

you a little about what I have learned, hoping this will lead you to make wise choices. My only concern is your health and safety.

When people talk about "drugs," they are generally referring to illegal substances such as marijuana, cocaine, methamphetamine (speed), psychedelic drugs (LSD, Ecstasy, "Schrooms") and heroin.

These are not the only drugs that make you high. Alcohol, cigarettes and many other substances (like glue) cause intoxication of some sort. The fact that one drug or another is illegal does not mean one is better or worse for you. All of them temporarily change the way you perceive things and the way you think.

Some people will tell you that drugs feel good, and that's why they use them. But drugs are not always fun. Cocaine and methamphetamine speed up your heart; LSD can make you feel disoriented; alcohol intoxication impairs driving; cigarette smoking leads to addiction and sometimes lung cancer; and people sometimes die suddenly from taking heroin. Marijuana does not often lead to physical dependence or overdose, but it does alter the way people think, behave and react.

Reasons to Avoid Drugs

I have tried to give you a short description of the drugs you might encounter. I choose not to try to scare you by distorting information because I want you to have confidence in what I tell you. Although I won't lie to you about their effects, there are many reasons for a person your age to not use drugs or alcohol.

First, being high on marijuana or any other drug often interferes with normal life. It is difficult to retain information while high, so using it, especially daily, affects your ability to learn.

Second, if you think you might try marijuana, please wait until you are older. Adults with drug problems often started using at a very early age.

Finally, your father and I don't want you to get into trouble. Drug and alcohol use is illegal for you, and the consequences of

NORML fights to legalize marijuana and to help those who have been convicted and sentenced for possessing or selling marijuana. It believes that adults (but not minors) should have the freedom to decide whether to use marijuana. NORML publishes pamphlets and position papers on both marijuana and drug policy, and the monthly magazine *Potpourri*.

Websites

ClubDrugs.org
www.clubdrugs.org

A service of the National Institute on Drug Abuse (NIDA), this website provides research and facts about club drugs like MDMA (Ecstasy), GHB, Rohypnol, ketamine, methamphetamine, and LSD.

Dear Lucie
www.lucie.com

Lucie Walters writes a syndicated newspaper and online advice column for teens called Adolessons. Her columns discuss drug and alcohol abuse, as well as other topics that concern teens. Visitors to the site can read archives of her column as well as participate in message boards and chat rooms.

DrugHelp.org
www.drughelp.org

The website provides information and referrals to drug abuse treatment facilities, self-help groups, and crisis centers throughout the United States.

ForReal.org

www.forreal.org

This website, created by the Center for Substance Abuse Prevention (CSAP), a federal agency, is designed to be an informative and entertaining source of information on the risks and harms marijuana can pose to the daily lives of teens.

KidsHealth

www.kidshealth.org

KidsHealth is one of the largest sites on the Internet providing doctor-appproved health information about children from before birth through adolescence. The website provides teens with information on drugs, addiction, and treatment.

Teen Advice Online (TAO)

www.teenadviceonline.org

TAO's teen counselors from around the world offer advice for teens on drugs and addiction, as well as relationships, dating, sex, and other issues. Teens can submit questions to the counselors or read about similar problems in the archives.

Index